THE BELL TOLLS, NO ECHO:
Soldiers Who Can't Go Home

Thomas Y. Chung

Translated by John H. Cha

ISBN-13: 9781798771655

DEDICATION

This book is dedicated to all those brave soldiers who gave their body and soul to their country and fellow brothers and sisters.

CONTENTS

Nomenclatures:

DPRK	Democratic People's Republic of Korea aka North Korea
ICC	International Criminal Court (The Hague)
KPA	[North] Korean People's Army
NATO	North Atlantic Treaty Organization
PRC	Peoples Republic of China, aka Chicom
PVA	Peoples Volunteer Army (aka PRC Army)
ROK	Republic of Korea aka South Korea
ROKA	Republic of Korea Army aka South Korean Army
UN	United Nations
UNC	United Nations Command
UNGA	United Nations General Assembly
UNSC	United Nations Security Council
UNCURK	United Nations Commission for the Unification and Rehabilitation of Korea
US	United States
USFK	United States Forces-Korea

FOREWORD

One busy day in Los Angeles in 1994, I was struck by a scene on a Korean TV program. A man fully dressed in the familiar Korean army uniform donning an old lieutenant's insignia stood at attention. Looking to be over seventy years old, he was nothing but skin and bones. He saluted to an officer much younger than him, shouting, "Serial number XXXXX, army Lieutenant Cho XX reporting to duty, sir!"

Intrigued, I continued to watch the program to hear him say, "I had been a POW in North Korea for a long time. I escaped North Korea and returned to my homeland South Korea after forty years." The gentleman's name was Cho Chang-ho. He continued, "Many POWs still remain incarcerated in North Korea, POWs who live under duress."

A veteran of the Korean War serving the South Korean Army, I always surmised that all the POWs from respective nations had been returned to their homes. But here was Lieutenant Cho saying that there were many POWs still remaining in North Korea. I was appalled.

At the same time, I started to think about my old army buddies who had been missing since the war, my subordinates, my communication officer, and my friends from my old hometown. I thought they might be among those POWs that Lieutenant Cho was referring to. Hence, I founded the Committee for Repatriation of POWs to free and bring the POWs home.

I started to visit legislators in Washington DC and Seoul and talked to them about freeing these POWs. I pleaded with any political figure who I thought might be interested, as well as the media. Ten years have passed since I started this campaign.
During that time, eighty-one former POWs have escaped from North Korea on their own. We have not managed to rescue any from incarceration ourselves, and I feel ashamed. Despite the considerable

effort and expenses over the ten years, I must confess that we have not been able to penetrate the thick door to the POWs.

When the Korean War that began with North Korea's invasion of the South, many young men of South Korea answered the call to defend the homeland. Unfortunately, many of them had become prisoners of war and spent their entire lives in North Korea, enduring all kinds of oppression and contempt. It hurts me to imagine them waiting and hoping for their nation to rescue them all those years. Many of them perished, never realizing their dream of going home.

Having had my own experiences of escaping from life-and-death situations, I sometimes imagine myself as a POW looking at the southern sky and wondering if my country would come and rescue me. I have written this book for my comrades and warriors who were and are imprisoned in North Korea. I want to let the world know why they didn't make it back home and to give ourselves an opportunity to reflect on our failure to bring them all home.

I want to thank all those who helped me with the work of the Committee for the Repatriation of POWs, Mr. Hong-jin Byun (Tom Byun), who had been my shadow for the past ten years as the general manager, Chairman Bong-gun Kim of Veterans Association Western Branch, Mr. Han-hoi Kim who has dealt with all the legal matters with ICC (International Criminal Court) and UN Human Rights Committee, and Mr. Gyu-bok Hwang who has helped with collecting data and material.

Also, I want to thank all the board members including Dr. Chang-gyu Park who has always encouraged me.

My heartfelt love and thanks go to my wife who patiently supported me through the committee work despite the financial burden.
My prayers to my comrades in arms who have gone before me.

Thomas Y. Chung, an old soldier

MAP OF KOREA

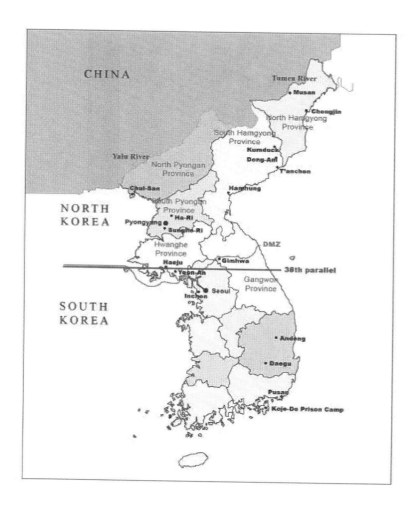

Chapter 1
THE KOREAN WAR BREAKS OUT

As I mentioned in the Foreword, the POW issue in the Korean peninsula is a complex one. Let me start with a question—how did the Korean War start? First, let's briefly talk about what was going on around the world at the time.

A. Korean War and International Situation

The world had gone through two world wars—WWI from 1914 to 1919 and WWII from 1939 to 1945. European nations, Eastern Europe, especially, and East Asia were struggling in extreme poverty.

Enter the Communist International (Comintern) movement founded by Vladimir Lenin in Moscow in March 1919 following the October Revolution (Bolshevik Revolution, 1917), which led to the creation of a new socialist nation USSR (1924-1991). The communist movement spread among the poverty-stricken countries in eastern Europe and Asia, including China. When Mao Zedong succeeded in forming the communist government, PRC (People's Republic of China), in 1949, 50% of the world population and territory became communist.

As for the Korean peninsula, it became liberated from the 35-year-long Japanese colonial rule on August 15, 1945, owing to the victory by the US and the allied forces in the Pacific War over imperial Japan. But the peninsula became divided in two along the 38th Parallel—the Soviet troops occupying the North, and the US troops in the South.

Subsequently, the North immediately came under the communist rule. The Soviet leader Joseph Stalin installed Kim Il-sung, then a captain in the Soviet army under the Fareast Command, as the leader of North Korea.

At the same time, the South sought to adopt a free, democratic system styled after the US system. However, the pro-communist forces supported by some intellectuals and poor farmers pursued the communist system for the South as well, initiating violent insurrections and disruptions.

The United Nations became involved in settling the governance of the Korean peninsula and called for a general election encompassing all the Korean population, north and south. The Soviets refused to participate in the general election, and the South went ahead with the election under the UN supervision. On August 15, 1948, the Republic of Korea (ROK) was founded in South Korea, electing Syngman Rhee as its first President. Thus, the UN General Assembly (UNGA) recognized ROK as the official government of the Korean peninsula on December 12, 1948.

With the founding of ROK, the pro-communist factions gradually faded and went underground. The South Korean situation seemed to have settled down on the surface, but the shadow of the communist pressure emanating from the vast Asian continent appeared too formidable for the Korean peninsula. With the advent of the Acheson Declaration[1] made by the US on January 12, 1950, which had excluded

---

[1] EXCERPTS FROM ACHESON'S SPEECH TO THE NATIONAL PRESS CLUB, JANUARY 12, 1950: "This defensive perimeter runs along the Aleutians to Japan and then goes to the Ryukyus. We hold important defense positions in the Ryukyu Islands, and those we will continue to hold. In the interest of the population of the Ryukyu Islands... from Ryukyus to the Philippine Islands..."JANUARY 12, 1950: "This defensive perimeter runs along the Aleutians to Japan and then goes to the Ryukyus. We hold important defensive positions in the Ryukyu Islands, and those we will continue to hold. In the interest of

Taiwan and South Korea from the defensive perimeter for the Pacific region, questions arose whether the US would help defend South Korea in the event that a war broke out. There is much debate about the Acheson Line. Miles Maochun Yu, a research fellow at Hoover Institute at Stanford University writes:

"On January 12, 1950, Secretary of State Dean Acheson gave a well-crafted speech at the National Press Club, a speech which has lived in infamy since its delivery, still haunting the U.S. and its allies in the Asia and Pacific region in general and the Korean Peninsula in particular.

To most people, this was a veritable green light given by Mr. Acheson to the communists to invade South Korea on June 25, 1950. The speech is remembered for its crucial element: the exclusion of the Republic of Korea [South Korea] and the Republic of China [Taiwan] from a U.S. "defense perimeter" that runs from Japan's Ryukyu Islands to the Philippines. This reduced American "defense perimeter" encouraged communist forces in North Korea to take military actions without suffering American military reprisals, a key concern of Joseph Stalin, Mao Zedong, and Kim Il-sung prior to Acheson's speech. According to Soviet eyewitness accounts made available after the Soviet Union's collapse in the early 1990s, Acheson's speech was rushed to Stalin's desk for a careful study. Stalin then immediately held secret deliberations with Mao, who had been in the USSR since late December 1949, about the seemingly changed military assessment concerning Korea. Ever since Moscow created the Democratic People's Republic of Korea [North Korea] in 1948, Kim had been begging Stalin to approve his plan to attack South Korea, only to be repeatedly rejected by him on account of an assumed American military response. But only two weeks after Acheson's speech, as the post-Soviet Union archival releases have indicated, on January 30, 1950, Stalin finally issued a general approval for Kim Il-sung to launch the attack on the South."

---

the population of the Ryukyu Islands… from Ryukyus to the Philippine Islands…"

Residents of Seoul escape on a wooden boat after the Han River bridge was destroyed. June 28, 1950.

By the end of July 1950, the North Korean army occupied 90% of South Korea except the Nakdong defensive line.

Women refugees along the road southward. July 1950

B. From SoJon to Nakdong River

Sunday morning on June 25, 1950, North Korean forces (KPA) made a surprise attack, led by Soviet-made tanks and fighter planes at 4:00am in the eastern front and 2:00am in the middle front. It was a well-coordinated campaign, involving 242 pieces of T-34/85 tanks, 58 pieces of type-74 tanks, 200 Yak fighters and bombers, and 231,000 troops under cover of all types of field artillery equipment.

South Korea's manpower stood at 98,000 troops, of which 65,000 were combat troops. Most of the South Korean soldiers had been on leave the day before, helping with rice planting in their hometowns. The remaining forces tried to fight off the charge, but they were overrun by the superior North Korean forces. The South Korean capital city Seoul fell into the communist hands just in three days on June 28, 1950.

The South Korean army, without warning, blew up and destroyed the Han River bridge at 2:30am on June 28 to slow down the North Korean charge. Consequently, many South Korean troops were trapped on the north side of the river and taken prisoner.

A refugee family on foot. Aug 7, 1950

Shoeshine boys in the rear region. Aug 7, 1950

A line of refugees with loaded ox carts. Aug 7, 1950

At the time, Seoul's population was approximately 1.45 million, and only 400,000 people had managed to make it to the south side of the river. The North Korean army did not pursue the fleeing South Korean troops across the river right away. Instead, they remained in Seoul until June 30th due to the resistance by the South Korean 6th Army positioned around ChoonChun, led by Colonel KIM Jong-ho. The North Korean advance was delayed by three days, and this was a massive help for the allied forces in establishing a defense line at the Nakdong River. The enemy lost its chance to cross the Nakdong River and gave the UN allied forces an opportunity to turn around the momentum.

At this point, we need to take a look at why the South Korean forces were defeated so quickly at the outset. As I have mentioned before, the peninsula had been divided, and during the process, a number of communist sympathizers infiltrated the South in all sectors of the society, including the military.

The South Korean army command system failed to assess the situation concerning the North's surprise attack because the enemy personnel had disabled the communication network, according to evidentiary materials found later.

For instance, a staff member named Lieutenant Ra Uhm-gwang who served the Army Chief of Staff Chai Byung-duk turned out to be a member of Namrodang (Southern Workers [Communist] Party), not a member of the South Korean military. He disappeared on the day the war began. He had blocked all the reports to Army Chief of Staff Chai.

Here are some examples:

- On June 10th, fifteen days before the invasion, all the heavy equipment and trucks were moved to BuPyung factory for repair, and they were not available for combat duty during the onslaught.

- On June 15th, ten days before the invasion, there were massive personnel changes among the rank and file, causing great confusion in the command system.

- On June 24th, all the troops on duty were given furloughs. On the evening of June 24th, a party was held for the top brass, who drank and danced late into the night.

Accordingly, the enemy infiltration had disabled the South Korean army from reacting to the invasion.

C. The UN Enters the War

With the advent of the war, South Korean President Syngman Rhee instructed Ambassador Chang Myun and his secretary Han Pyo-ok to file a report to the US Department of the State. The UN issued UNG #293 to cease all fighting in the Korean peninsula, followed by UN Security Council Resolution UNSC #82 to stop all fight.

However, the North Korean army ignored the resolution and continued to march southward, and the UN issued UNSC #83 to warn the North Korean forces to withdraw to the north of the 38th Parallel. But again the North Korean troops ignored the resolution and continued to march southward.

As UNSC #83 came into being, the 33rd US President Harry S. Truman directed General Douglas MacArthur, the Supreme Commander of UN Fareast Command, to provide naval and air support for South Korea immediately.

Thus the 7th Fleet was dispatched to Taiwan Straight to protect Taiwan. General MacArthur boarded an airplane from the Haneda airport in Japan on June 29th to examine the defensive situation in Korea and immediately requested reinforcement troops.

> Truman later wrote in his memoir, "Communism was acting in Korea just as Hitler, Mussolini, and the Japanese had acted ten, fifteen, and twenty years earlier. I felt certain that if South Korea were allowed to fall, Communist leaders would be encouraged to override nations closer to our own shores. If the Communists were permitted to force their way into the Republic of Korea without opposition from the free world, no small nation would have the courage to resist threats and aggression by stronger Communist neighbors. If this were allowed to go unchallenged, it would mean a third world war, just as similar incidents had brought on the Second World War. It was also clear to me that the foundations and the principles of the United Nations were at stake unless this unprovoked attack on Korea could be stopped."[2]

Meanwhile, ROK President Syngman Rhee dispatched a letter to the UN Supreme Command to transfer the command of ROKA (ROK Army) to the UN Supreme Command on July 14, and on July 17, General MacArthur accepted the authority.

The UN Security Council requested to the members of the UN for support troops in order to stop North Korea from continuing with the

---

[2] Truman, Harry S., *Years of Trial and Hope* (1956), vol. 2, pp. 331-333.

invasion and passed Resolution #84 to establish the UNC (UN Command).

British troops board a ship to Korean War.

Sixteen member nations joined the UNC in addition to ROKA, and the UN Security Council issued Resolution #85 naming General MacArthur as the Supreme Commander of the UNC. Thus, the Korean War became a war between the UNC led by the US forces versus the North Korean People's Army (KPA). Later in 1951, the PRC (People's Republic of China) army joined North Korea in the war.

D. Inchon Landing Operation and Nakdong Defense Line

1. Nakdong River defense line:
    Having penetrated the 38th Parallel on June 25, the North Korean KPA occupied Seoul on June 28th, Osan on July 5th, Daejon on July 24th, Mokpo and Jinju at the end of July, KimChun and Pohang by early August. The enemy planned to reach Busan (Pusan) by way of Daegu (Taegu) and applied tremendous pressure, but the UNC and ROKA stood ground at the Nakdong River. General PAIK Sun-yop, commander of

ROKA 1st Division, was instrumental in defending Daegu and turned the table around at the DaBuDong battle and tied the enemy down to an impasse.

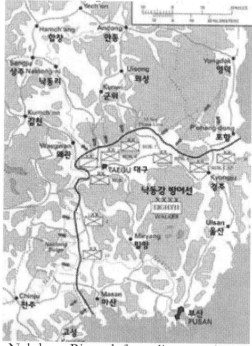

Nakdong River defense line, southeast corner of the peninsula. Aug 1950

2. Inchon Landing Operation:

With the enemy forces locked in an impasse at the Nakdong line, General MacArthur came up with a plan to counter the enemy with a fatal blow by landing in Inchon to cut off the enemy supply line at its waist. He proposed his idea to Pentagon, but Pentagon was concerned about the severe tidal condition in Inchon and suggested a landing in Gunsan. General MacArthur insisted on Inchon and got President Truman to agree. In a coordinated campaign with a counter-offensive at Nakdong River, the Inchon land operation was carried out.

US Air Force bombers cut off the enemy
supply line. Aug 16, 1950

General Douglas MacArthur directs the Inchon landing operation.
September 15, 1950

The X Corps comprised of the 1st Marine Division and the 7th Division and 5,000 ROKA marines landed on Wolmido at full tide at dawn on September 15 under the code name of Operation Chromite. They recovered the city of Inchon the next day, entered Seoul on September 26th, and recaptured the capital by September 28 in three months.

General MacArthur on his way to inspect the front.

ROKA troops raise South Korean flag at Seoul central government office. September 26, 1950

UNC troops attend a mass at the footsteps of Seoul Central Government building. September 28, 1950

As the result of the counter-offensive by the UNC, the enemy forces lost 13 divisions in mere 15 days, and 23,000 enemy troops became POWs in the hands of ROKA or UNC, with Chief of Staff LEE Hak-gu[3] among them.

KPA Colonel Lee Hak-gu as POW at Koje Island POW camp.

---

[3] LEE Hak-gu, the Chief of Staff for the KPA 13th Division killed his superior officer General HONG Yong-jin who had insisted on fighting to the last man. Subsequently, Colonel Lee proceeded to carry out a retreat for the division, when he was captured. He was the highest ranking North Korean POW. He was the ringleader for the POWs at Koje Island. When he was returned to the North after the war, he was punished for inciting a mutiny.

Those enemy troops that had been bogged down at Nakdong River retreated northward when their supply line was cut after the Inchon landing since the majority of the KPA remnants were destroyed during their retreat behind the 38th Parallel. On the other hand, the UNC forces lost around 18,000 troops.

The UNC forces reached the 38th Parallel by September 29th and held their position. They didn't advance further because the UN Security Council resolution was based on a defensive approach. However, the UN's ultimate mission was unification as well, and a fierce debate about advancing beyond the 38th Parallel ensued.

President Syngman Rhee who had been advocating unification by pushing northward insisted, "If we don't complete the unification at this time, we will be facing another horrible war like this, so despite all the hardship, we must use this opportunity to unify the nation." There didn't seem to be any other way than a military unification at the time.

So, President Rhee then summoned the ROKA Chief of Staff Chung Il-kwon and directed him to push northward by ROKA alone. General Chung went to General Walker, the commander of the US 8th army, and agreed to have ROKA take KamJe hill near KiSaMoon-ri, located at the north side of the 38th Parallel along the eastern front, because of its strategic value.[4]

ROKA 1st Corps comprised of the Capital Division and 3rd Division broke through the 38th Parallel on October 1st and recaptured YangYang and continued to advance northward. Meanwhile, the UN General Assembly adopted Resolution 376 (V) on October 7, 1950, establishing the United Nations Commission for the Unification and Rehabilitation of Korea (UNCURK) to "represent the United Nations in bringing about the establishment of a unified, independent and democratic government of all Korea."

On the western front, the US 1st Corps began advancing toward the ChungJu-YoungWon-HamHeung line. ROKA 1st Division led by General Paik Sun-yop entered Pyongyang on October 19th.

---

[4] "Korean War and ROK Army University School," ROK Army University Veterans Association, p.203

ROKA troops enter Pyongyang. October 25, 1950

About this time, President Truman and General MacArthur had a meeting at Wake Island on October 15th, when General MacArthur told President Truman, "We can destroy the enemy by November, by Christmas at the latest. We will leave just the X Corps in Korea, and the 8th Army can return to Japan."

President Truman expressed his concern about PRC (People's Republic of China), whether it would intervene or not. MacArthur told him that there was no worry, and that had PRC entered the war in the beginning, they would have made a difference, but there was no chance of it now. About 100,000 to 120,000 PRC troops were stationed along the Yalu River in Manchuria, and only 50,000 to 60,000 would have crossed the river.

MacArthur stepped up the advance to finish out the war as quickly as possible per his promise with President Truman. On October 17 when the US 8th Army was near Pyongyang, the UN Command order that had limited the advance to the ChungJu-YoungWon-HamHeung line was revised to SunChun-KoIn-Pyongyang-PoongSan-SungJin line, closer to the border. On October 24, the UN Command did away with this limiting line altogether and ordered all the units to approach the Chinese border at will.

ROKA 2nd Corps comprised of the 6th, 7th, and 8th Divisions pushed up to PakChun-TaiChun-WoonSan-OnJung-HuiChun line. The 7th

Regiment of the 6th Division led by commander Kim Jong-oh took ChoSan by the Yalu River and installed the South Korean flag *tageukki* on the shore. That was 2:15 pm on October 26th.

A strange thing happened the day before, though. ROKA 1st Division north of WoonSan captured a PRC infantryman. On the following day, ROKA 2nd Corps engaged an undetermined group of PRC personnel in a fierce firefight. Thus, they knew the PRC had entered the Korean theater for sure.

Captured North Korean POWs await new gear.

E. PRC Campaigns

PRC Premier Zhou Enlai warned the UN on August 20, 1950: "Korea is a neighboring country, so China can enter the Korean War because of China' safety."[5]

On October 1, 1950, the anniversary date of Mao Zedong's defeat of Chiang Kai-shek, the Soviet ambassador in Peking delivered a letter from Joseph Stalin to Mao and Zhou Enlai requesting them to provide reinforcement for North Korea to the tune of five to six divisions.[6]
Kim Il-sung pleaded with Mao for reinforcement as well.

Accordingly, PRC held a high-level conference regarding military and political affairs and appointed Lin Biao to take charge of the troops for the Korean theater, but Lin declined the appointment on account of his health. So, Peng Dehuai took the field command with Zhou Enlai taking the overall responsibility.

Mao renamed the northeast territory (dongbei) defense forces as People's Volunteer Army (PVA) on October 8th and decided to inject the troops into the Korean theater. On October 10th, he met with Joseph Stalin who had been vacationing at the Black Sea and requested for military support and received promises of equipment and ammunition.[7]

Thus the Chinese troops began to cross the Yalu (Apnok) River on the night of October 19th. The Chinese PVA forces moved at night, usually from 1900 hours to 0300 hours to avoid detection by the UN's aerial surveillance. They were a well-trained group, traveling 286 miles from Dandong to the battlefront in 19 days, averaging about 18 miles a day over and around the mountainous terrains.

---

[5] Stokesbury, James L., *A Short History of the Korean War*, (New York, Harper Perennial, 1990), p.83
[6] Barnouin, Barbara & Yu, Changgeng, *Zhou Enlai: A Political Life*, (Hong Kong, Chinese University Press, 2006), p. 144
[7] David Halberstam, *The Coldest Winter: America and the Korean War* (New York, Hyperion, 2007), p. 361

Chinese troops cross the Yalu River. October 1950

At this point, the UNC experienced difficulty in communication between the western front and the eastern front. After the successful landing at Inchon, General Edward Almond's X Corps consisting of the 1st Marine Division sailed around the south of the peninsula and landed on the eastern coast of Korea at Wonsan, unopposed.

Trouble was that they couldn't communicate with the 8th Army at the western front led by General Walker. This allowed the PRC forces to infiltrate the central territory left open in between the 8th and the X Corps.

This mistake could be attributed to General MacArthur. Many military historians believe that had the 8th Army been given the responsibility for the overall command strategy, the X Corps would have fallen under the single command structure led by the 8th Army, which would have facilitated for smoother communication and prevented the massive PRC infiltration. As a result, the UNC could have avoided the defeat at Chosin Reservoir.

We need to take a look at the reasons for the Chinese intervention at this point. The Chinese army personnel had been recovering from the civil war which ended in 1949, yet Mao decided to participate in the war. He had two reasons.

One, if the communist forces collapsed in North Korea, the Americans would come right up to the Chinese border. Mao wanted a buffer zone between the US and China.

Two, it is not historically well known, but the most important reason for entering the Korean War was the fact that Mao was having difficulty dealing with the 1.5 million prisoners from his civil war with Chiang Kaishek's nationalist army.

In addition, the Korean War presented Mao an opportunity to dispatch the prisoners and resolve the problem within the military ranks. At the same time, this was an opportunity for Mao to bolster his solidarity with his allies, mainly the Soviets and North Koreans, as well as removing the US forces from North Korea.

This question of the origin of the PVA forces came to light during the POW exchange process which was part of the armistice agreement between the PRC and the UN after the Korean War. The PRC command tried to direct all the POWs to return to China, but the POWs refused to go to mainland China. Instead, the POWs with nationalist origin insisted on going to Taiwan, where the nationalist, non-communist government was seated.

The UN side agreed with the nationalist POWs, and the PRC side decided to send these POWs to Taiwan. This POW incident surrounding the Chinese POWs proved that a good portion of the Chinese troops in the Korean War was of nationalist origin. It is an ironic twist of fate that set non-communist Chinese forces against non-communist Korean soldiers during the war.

1. **PRC Forces' First Wave Assault**

The PRC 13th Army began its first campaign on October 19th. Its 40th Army attacked ROKA 6th Division of the 2nd Corps on October 25th, while the PRC 39th Army took on ROKA 1st Division.

This was the second day after ROKA and the UNC forces crossed the ChungChun River, and the advance troops from ROKA 6th Regiment moved from HoeMokDong to GoJang around 60 km south of the border. The MacArthur line, SunChun-GoIn-Pyongyang-PoongSan-SungJin line, had been discarded on October 24th.

When the PRC 2nd Army attacked the ROKA 6th Division of the 2nd Corps on October 25th, a part of the enemy forces had arrived north of ChungChun River, WoonSan and OnJung, cutting off the path of ROKA 6th Division, the 1st Division, and the 7th Regiment of the 6th Division. The ROKA personnel were overwhelmed by the PRC forces closing in on them from all directions.

The UN Command mistook the scale of the PRC campaign, calling it "mere reinforcement personnel stationed along the river as border guards."

The UNC rushed the US 1st Cavalry Division to WoonSan past ROKA 1st Division and had the US 1st Corps to continue to advance toward the border region between Sinuiju and SooPoong.

On the eastern front, ROKA 1st Corps and the US 10th Corps continued to push toward the China border while they had no contact with the PRC forces.[8] But the operation by the 1st Mechanized Division failed, and the UNC/ROKA forces near WoonSan had to retreat.

---

[8] Silok (The Chronicles), Korean War and Army University School, p.232

The PRC's first wave from October 25th to November 5th, comprised of the 38th, the 39th, and the 40th Army, with 30,000 infantrymen each. They were highly skilled veterans.

The PRC's surprise appearance collapsed the balance of the frontline of the US 8th Army, threatening the exit route for the units which had advanced to JungGoDong. The UNC had the units retreat 90 km on or about November 1st and formed a new defense line on the southern shore of the ChungChun River and made ready to recover.

When the PRC troops reached the river sometime between November 5th and November 7th, they began to retreat to the mountainside rather than engaging. On the eastern front, ROKA's 26th Regiment of the 3rd Division had an encounter with the PRC infantry along the small canyon in SooDong and retreated.

Sometime later, ROKA 1st Corps and the US X Corps paused their advance near ChangJinHo-PoongSan-SungJin line and waited for orders. This was when they confirmed the appearance of the PRC tanks.

Here are the major encounters in the PRC's first-wave assault:

- OnJung-ri battle (25OCT50 – 28OCT50), ROKA 6th Division, 2nd Regiment, and 19th Regiment; ROKA 7th Division, 10th Regiment
- WoonSan battle (25OCT50 – 28OCT50), US 1st Cavalry Division; ROKA 1st Division
- BiHoSan/GoonWoo-ri battle (02NOV50 – 04NOV50), British Commonwealth Forces (BCFK) Division
- HyeSanJin battle (21NOV50), Eastern front US 10th Corps, 7th Division, 17th, and 20th Regiment

PRC troops counter attack in GaeChun. November 1950

2. **PRC Forces' Second Wave Assault**

PRC 13th Army group destroyed ROKA 2nd Corps at the Chungchun River battle on the western front on November 25th and drove back the US 2nd Infantry Division at the right flank. Thus began the longest retreat operation in the history of the US Army. Thanks to the brave Turkish brigade that held back the advancing PRC units and made the retreat operation possible from November 27th to the 29th.

PRC troops cheer their victory after the ChangJinHo (Chosin) battle, December 1950.

Escape from ChangJinHo (Chosin Reservoir)

On the eastern front, about 3,000 infantrymen in the US 7th Infantry Division and the 1st Marines Division (12,000 – 15,000 men) were caught encircled in a 3-day siege by the PRC 9th Army, losing about 15,000 troops.

Called the "Battle of Chosin," this combat marked the most casualties suffered in the US military history. It is called Chosin because it is the Japanese pronunciation of the Korean word Changjin, and remained as Chosin on maps. Those troops who had managed to make it out of the area were aptly named "Chosin Few."

The US 1st Marine Division was nearly wiped out, and the survivors escaped to Hungnam and withdrew to the South aboard ships. Subsequently, the PRC 13th Army group drove away from the 8th Army by November 30th and pushed them back to the 38th Parallel by mid-December.

Meanwhile, on the eastern front, the US X Corps delayed the PRC 9th Army group and succeeded in building the HungNam defensive perimeter, setting the ground for the famous HungNam evacuation operation.

Refugees gather at HungNam dock. December 19, 1950

HungNam Evacuation Operation

The US 9th Corps and the X Corps mobilized in the port city of Hungnam and retreated southward on ships. The evacuation operation involved 105,000 troops, 98,000 civilian refugees, 17,500 pieces of mobile vehicles, and 350,000 tons of supplies and equipment shipped on 193 ships to Pusan.

The ROKA personnel who had retreated from the north had assembled at Hungnam port as well. All the confusion and melee necessitated General Kim Baik-il to issue an order for all the ROKA personnel to evacuate on foot to make more room for civilian evacuees.

Refugees crowd HungNam port to board the UN cargo ship.
December 19, 1950.

The most famous ship in association with Hungnam evacuation is SS Meredith Victory, which was the last ship to leave the port. Built in 1945, she was a 7,600-ton US Merchant Marine Victory cargo ship with room for 60 passengers including 47 crew members, which left room for only 13 passengers.

The dock was crowded with people, vehicles, mounds of goods, and troops in a melee, and they all needed to be loaded onto the last ship to Pusan. SS Meredith Victory was there to load the equipment and the troops, with no room for civilians.

Commander of the X Corps Lt. General Edward M. Almond had no choice but to leave the refugees on the dockside. As the civilian refugees wailed and clamored for passage to safety, then General Almond's advisor Dr. Bong-hak Hyun told the general, "Our military mission is to fight for freedom and democracy, and how could we leave behind these people who want to go to free, democratic nation in the hands of the enemy?" He pleaded with the general to bring the civilians along. ROKA advisor of civilian affairs Colonel Yu Won-shik also pleaded with General Almond and his staff officers to save the civilians. General Almond relented and made the decision to unload the military equipment and make room for the civilians. But it was impossible to take all the civilians on the 7,600-ton cargo ship.

Captain Leonard P. LaRue[9] (1914-2001) made the decision to load all the civilians "even if the ship sank." He ordered the civilians to discard all the bags and luggage and let 14,000 civilians board the ship.

With the ship loaded beyond her capacity, Captain LaRue's ship crawled its way, arriving at the Pusan port 450 sea miles away on December 24th after 28 hours of the harrowing voyage.

He later recalled, "The refugees were packed like sardines in a can, and most had to remain standing up, shoulder-to-shoulder, in freezing weather conditions during the entire voyage, there were no injuries or casualties on board. There was very little food or water, and the people were virtually unable to move."

The port of Pusan refused to let her dock, though, citing that the port was overrun with refugees. Captain LaRue had to go another 50 miles

---

[9] Captain Leonard P. LaRue was born in Philadelphia and spent 22 years at sea. He retired in 1954 and entered the Benedictine monastery St. Paul's Abbey in Newton, New Jersey. He lived out his life as Brother Marinius serving the needy until 2001. Then the Staff Officer J. Robert Lunney and Ahn Jae-chul registered SS Meredith Victory as the "largest evacuation from land by a single ship." The ship was broken up and sold to China as scrap metal in 1993. Its model is displayed at Long Beach, California.

to KoJe Island and dock at the tiny port of JangSeungPo on Christmas Day, 1950.

Years later, Captain LaRue reflected, "I often think of that voyage. I think of how such a small vessel was able to hold so many persons and surmount endless perils without harm to a soul. And, as I think the clear, unmistakable message come to me that on that Christmastide, in the bleak and bitter waters off the shores of Korea, God's own hand was at the helm of my ship."

SS Meredith Victory was one of the few ships that received the title of "Gallant Ship" by the U.S. Congress and signed by President Dwight D. Eisenhower.

Refugees pack the US Merchant Marine ship SS Meredith Victory.
December 23, 1950

Meanwhile, the Commander of the 8th Army General Walton Walker was killed in a traffic accident on December 23rd, lowering the morale among the rank and file.

His replacement General Mathew Ridgway arrived in Korea on December 26 and focused on rebuilding the morale of the troops and replenishing equipment and supplies.

3. PRC Forces' Third Wave Assault

On the last day of 1950, the PRC forces pushed southward en-masse using superior manpower in the so-called human wave strategy, blowing flutes and pounding brass gongs, overpowering the UNC and the allied forces. On January 4, 1951, the capital city of Seoul fell into enemy hands once again.

Pushed below the 38th Parallel, General MacArthur suggested dropping an atomic bomb to cut off the supply line and the PRC personnel route, but the strategy was opposed by Washington fearing that it would start WW3. (The Soviets had tested its atomic weapon in 1949, but I agree with those experts who think that Washington had overestimated the Soviet's nuclear weapons at that time.)

General Ridgway focused on reviving the troops' morale and regrouped the units that had retreated to as far south as Suwon, WonJu, and Sam Chuk. He attacked the long enemy supply line and cut off the route for food and ammunition, slowly pushing the PRC forces back to WonJu.

PRC Commander Peng Dehuai is inspecting the front.

PRC troops attack US tank in the Gumhwa battle.

4. **PRC Forces' Fourth Wave Assault**

The PRC began its counteroffensive mid-February of 1951, with an attempt to take back HongChun by encircling the city with 25,000 troops. However, the US 2nd Infantry Division, French battalion, and ROKA personnel, altogether 5,600 troops, withstood the PRC siege and pushed them back in the first victory against the PRC forces since the PRC entered the war. The battle was coined the "Gettysburg of the Korean War," having been outnumbered five to one.

Thus the 8th Army gained momentum and countered with superior firepower, taking back Seoul on March 7, 1951. Seoul had changed hands four times now, and its population dropped from 1.5 million to about 200,000.

By this time, Mao Zedong had sent a letter (dated March 1) to Joseph Stalin and made an urgent request for air support to protect his supply line. Stalin answered Mao's request by agreeing to supply two air force divisions, three ground-to-air combat divisions, and 600 mobile vehicles.

Near the end of April, Peng Dehuai sent his deputy to Zhou Enlai and explained that the danger he was facing was not the enemy itself but "the lack of food and ammunition, much less the vehicles to transport the wounded back to the rear."

Zhou promised to take care of Peng's requests, but Zhou did not keep all of his promises. Zhou agreed to engage the PRC air force starting September 1951 to overcome the inferiority in air power.

Meanwhile, President Truman sacked General MacArthur on April 11th and replaced him with General Mathew Ridgway. General Van Fleet took command of the 8th Army.

Here were some reasons cited for General MacArthur's termination:

- A mistake in judgment was thinking that the PRC would not intervene when pushing beyond the 38th Parallel, thereby causing significant casualties.
- A mistake in assuming that employment of atomic weapons was within his authority.
- A difference of opinion. General MacArthur believed that a complete military victory was the only important result. On the other hand, Truman thought that a comprehensive victory in Asia was difficult and that it was better to call for a truce at an appropriate opportunity and withdraw the UN forces. Also, the communist powerbase was expanding across eastern Europe, necessitating reinforcement of NATO (established in 1949) to protect Europe. Truman didn't want to tie up the US forces in Korea any longer.
- Refusal to follow the Supreme Commander Truman's orders. Also, he never spent a night in Korea as the commander, and exercised his command in comfort from Japan.[10]

The enemy continued their attack after General MacArthur's termination and the arrival of General Ridgway and General Van Fleet.

Nevertheless, the UN forces managed to push them back in coordination with the air support. They trapped the PRC forces between Seoul and KaeSung and pounded them. The UN forces advanced northward past the 38th Parallel to the so-called "Kansas Line." Then the PRC units reorganized their front around mid-April and began a new assault in May in its 5th Spring Season Assault.

---

[10] Stokesbury, James L., *A Short History of the Korean War*, (New York, Harper Perennial, 1990), p. 123-127; Stein, Conrad R., *The Korean War: "The Forgotten War,"* (Hillside, NJ, Enslow, 1994), p. 69, p. 79; Halberstam, David, *The Coldest Winter: America and the Korean War*, (New York, Hyperion, 2007), p. 498, p. 600

5. PRC Forces' Fifth Assault and Failure

Come April, the PRC forces mobilized a group consisting of three corps, totaling 270,000 strong and began attacking the US 1st Army from ImJin River and GaPyung.

By May, the PRC had attacked the Kansas Line and occupied it. The UN forces launched a counteroffensive at the end of May, and retook the Kansas Line and held it. This was the beginning of the impasse. The ensuing battles did little to the configuration of the overall front line, as most of the actions took place on a battalion level skirmishes.

Basically, the UNC reinforced bombing missions above the 38th Parallel to keep the PRC in check. The impasse caused the communist forces to give up its dream to turn the entire peninsula into a communist state. On the other hand, the impasse put up more distance to the UN's mission to unify the peninsula as a free democratic nation.

PRC forces in the fifth assault campaign. May 195

PRC artillery units are getting ready for the Spring assault. May 1951

LOOMING TALK OF TRUCE

On June 23, 1951, Mr. Jacob Malik, the Russian Ambassador to the United Nations, appeared in UN Broadcasting and mentioned a possibility of a truce on the radio. The U.S., despite the strong opposition by ROK President Syngman Rhee, accepted the suggestion from the Russian side.[11]

There were a number of reasons why the U.S. accepted the idea of the truce. Washington determined that more manpower was needed to achieve a complete military victory in the Korean peninsula, but the situation in Europe preempted the idea of reinforcing the manpower in the Fareast.

---

[11] Hermes, Walter, *Truce Tent, and Fighting Front: United States Army in the Korean War*, (Washington DC, US Army Center of Military History, 1992), p.15

The rapid spreading of communism was swallowing up impoverished Europe as an aftermath of the WWII, and this was a major concern for the U.S. policymakers who placed priority in Europe over the Fareast. As for the remaining UN coalition members, increasing their level of troop participation would overburden them.

In order to achieve the unification of the Korean peninsula, it was necessary to nullify the influential power of China, and this meant that the allied forces would have to go beyond the border and disable the PRC forces.

If the UN allied forces attempted to neutralize the PRC forces inside the PRC, the Soviet Union would not have sat still, opening the possibility of the WW3, and the U.S. could not risk that. So, the U.S. settled for preventing the communist forces from taking over the entire peninsula. Thus the UNC focused on a defensive strategy rather than attack mode.

PRC POWs are taking a break.

Consequently, after it smashed the PRC's Spring assault, the UNC strategy involved a defensive posture rather than advancement northward in unifying the peninsula. Thus, the UNC sought to occupy and hold positions that it deemed advantageous for defensive purpose, which led to fierce battles. These battles went on even during the truce talks.

South Korean President Syngman Rhee determined that the only way to unify the Koreas was thru military means and sought to advance northward. He felt that, as long as the communists had started the war, the free world should counter the aggression with resolve.

He called on General Chung Il-kwon, the Chief of Staff for ROKA, and directed him to make the northward push by ROKA alone. But that was impossible because ROKA belonged to the UN command led by the US 8th Army, and ROKA alone could not act on its own. Besides, a mission without the support of the US military forces was unthinkable.

Rhee's absolute opposition to the truce was legendary. He tried to disrupt the truce talks process any way he could and became a thorn in the US's side. He unilaterally freed the North Korean POWs in June 1953, which prompted the US to consider unseating him from his office.

Rhee refused to become a party to the truce, and ROK was not a signing member in the truce document. Rhee's fierce opposition to the truce provided some advantages for him during his negotiations with the U.S. in forging the ROK-USA alliance, as well as a commitment for a substantial financial aid in rebuilding South Korea.

Chapter 2
THE TRUCE NEGOTIATIONS

As I mentioned earlier, the Soviet's suggestion to the truce was accepted by the U.S. and the UN. They agreed to hold the first round of talks in KaeSung following an exchange of lists of participants and proposed agenda via respective communications offices.[12]

A. Selection of Agenda

The PRC's attitude toward the truce talks was as follows:
- Complete withdrawal of the UN forces from the Korean peninsula
- Return of Taiwan to PRC
- PRC to replace Taiwan as the official UN representative

---

[12] The meeting hall was moved to Panmunjom on October 24, 1951.

These conditions did not go over well with the U.S. side. The U.S. negotiators realized that they needed to exercise patience and continual military pressure in dealing with the PRC negotiators. The PRC's failed May assault campaign served as a reminder to all the parties that PRC would not be able to have its way through a military effort.

Given these conditions, the Soviet deputy minister of Foreign Affairs Andrei Gromyko communicated to the U.S. Ambassador Allen G. Kirk to leave the truce matter to the field commanders, and that political or territorial issue should be excluded from the truce talks.

General Ridgway appeared on a radio program and suggested that the truce talks should take place on the Danish hospital ship moored off the port of Wonsan and that they should set the date.

Working group from both sides.

The first location for the truce talks in KaeSung   NaeBongJang.
Changed to Panmunjom later.

On the same day, the U.S. State Department issued a directive to General Mathew Ridgway concerning Washington's overall approach to the truce, involving securing the truce and methods to prevent recurrence. There was to be no political discussions and negotiations, no mention of Taiwan, and no mention of replacing Taiwan as the UN representative. The truce talk should be limited to purely military matters and the establishment of a demilitarized zone of 20 miles from either side of the current battlefront.

The communist side (PRC, especially) responded with the following:

- Complete withdrawal of all foreign troops at the time of the truce; return of Taiwan to PRC;
- Replacement of Taiwan as the UN representative;
- 38th Parallel as the demarcation line;

- A demilitarized zone of 2km on either side of the 38th Parallel.

The difference was vast, and it appeared difficult for the parties to narrow the gap. Due to the UNC's continuous pressure by the superior air force and naval forces, the communist side relented on the points of withdrawal of all foreign troops, the Taiwan issue, and placing PRC in UN Security Council in place of Taiwan, on the basis that the truce talks should be limited to military affairs.

They eventually settled on the following:

- Agenda establishment
- Establishment of Demarcation Line and Demilitarized Zone
- Enacting terms of truce and control
- Discussion on the release of POWs

Of the items listed above, the establishment of the Demarcation Line, the Demilitarized Zone, and the POW exchange took the longest time. The reason the Korean War had lasted three years and one month was that they couldn't come to terms about the POW issue for over two years.

UN Truce talks representatives, Aug 13, 1951. From left, US General Henry Hodes, General Craigie, Admiral Turner Joy (Chief negotiator), ROKA General Paik Sun-yop, Admiral Arleigh Burke

Truce talks, communist side, July 16, 1951. From left, PRC General Hsieh Fang, PRC General Teng Hua, DPRK General Nam Il (Chief negotiator), DPRK General Lee Sang-jo, DPRK General Jang Pyung-san

B. <u>Demarcation Line Issue</u>

Negotiations concerning the Demarcation Line together with the POW problems were the most complex items in the truce talks because neither side was willing to give in. The communist coalition insisted that the 38th Parallel must be the demarcation line, while the UN persisted on the current battle line, as-is. The UN's position was rooted in configuring a demarcation line that served a defensive purpose if the communist forces ventured another invasion in the future.

The UN was not about to give up those hills they had fought so hard for, especially when they were not very adept at hillside combat, to begin with. The UN insisted on keeping the Kansas Line, the Wyoming Line[13], and the GumHwa-ChorWon-

---

[13] A defensive line set by General Van Fleet, Kansas Line starts from the mouth of ImJin River 20 miles north of Seoul toward GoRyangPo northeasterly past upper end of ImJin. Wyoming Line covers the mid-

PyungGang Line forming the "Iron Triangle" north of the 38th Parallel. The Iron Triangle, a rough, mountainous terrain, was crucial for defending against the enemy advance, and the UN forces had worked very hard to secure the area via fierce battles like "Bloody Ridge." The UN was not going to give up that position in any way.

Another problem was that KaeSung, so close to Seoul, was going to be placed north of the demarcation line. This was very disadvantageous for the UN side psychologically and politically. The UN negotiators tried to get KaeSung in exchange for positions in the mid-sector, but the communists did not go for the idea.

Both sides refused to budge on these issues, and the truce talks broke down. The UNC intensified its pressure on communist positions by calling up all the air force and naval power to bomb the major military facilities, the supply routes, Pyongyang, and industrial facilities, showing its resolve to the communist coalition that it wasn't giving in.

Ultimately, they settled to accept the current battle line as the demarcation line. Further, they agreed to retreat 2 km from the demarcation line, creating a 4 km-wide strip of land called the DMZ (demilitarized zone) across the waist of the peninsula.

C. POW Exchange

The POW exchange was a complicated issue right from the beginning. First of all, the definition of POWs was not clear, to begin with, and there was a problem with agreeing on the principle within the POW exchange procedure. Many scenarios were on the table, i.e., one-for-one exchange, all-for-all exchange, or Voluntary Repatriation[14] per the UN's suggestion.

eastern front from GoRyangPo to Iron Triangle.

[14] The reason the UN insisted on voluntary repatriation was that the most of the North Korean POWs had hailed from South Korea; and the PRC POWs were originally nationalist supporters of Chiang Kaishek. Nationalist supporters strongly refused to be repatriated to

They couldn't agree on any of these principles, with much difficulty in negotiations.

D. <u>South Korea's Unilateral Release of POWs</u>

Both sides struggled with the negotiations for months, and after a while, they were narrowing their differences in dealing with the POW issue. Once the POW issues were resolved, the truce was going to follow soon after.

Syngman Rhee, who firmly believed that unification had to happen now or never renewed his argument that the only way to achieve unification was by force. He insisted on stopping the truce negotiations. He wanted the UNC to push northward to defeat the communist coalition and unify the peninsula by force. If not the UNC, he insisted on ROKA to do it on its own.

But that was impossible because the war effort was under the US command, not to mention the weaponry and the supplies. Rhee had been trying to find ways to disrupt the truce negotiations. Right about that time, KPA POWs started an uprising at the KoJe POW camp, and South Korean military police took over the control of the camp.

As the truce negotiations were nearing the end around June 18, 1953, Rhee gave his commander of military police, General Chai Byung-duk, a secret order to release all the anti-communist POWs in eight camps across the country, except for the KoJe camp. The anti-communist POWs were reported to be 26,424 prisoners, but in actuality, they numbered at around 34,000.

---

communist China. North Korean POWs were divided into two groups: one group refused to be repatriated to Communist North (anti-communist POWs) while the other group (pro-communist POWs) preferred to be shipped to the North. These two groups of POWs fought each other to the point of producing many deaths. If the anti-communist POWs were sent to the North, they would face certain revenge and persecution. This was the biggest reason the UN side insisted on voluntary repatriation.

The North Korean truce negotiators strongly objected to the release. They demanded that the released POWs be returned and pulled out of the truce negotiation. (This incident could be why North Korea kept 78,636 South Korean POWs in North Korea without releasing them according to the terms of the truce.)

The US Air Force responded with an all-out attack on the North Korean supply route and military facilities. The North Korean truce negotiators returned to Panmunjom.

PRC POWs enjoy the warm spring weather at KoJe Island POW camp. March 20, 1953

Boys are cooking rice. March 1953

POW PROBLEMS IN PERSPECTIVE

In case of the American Independence War (American Revolutionary War) which took place between Great Britain and the thirteen colonies in America from 1775 to 1783, both sides declared that all POWs were free men at the Treaty of Paris. Thus, many British POWs chose to remain on the American continent. Accordingly, the POW exchange was not much of an issue.

After the WWII, the Soviet Union imprisoned a great number of POWs from Europe and Fareast and used them for recovery construction projects such as wells development projects in Siberia for many years.

Geneva Convention was instituted in 1929 to deal with the POW problems, followed by a revision in 1949, stating in clause 118 that all POWs must be returned to their respective home countries as soon as the hostilities terminate.

In reality, there were many difficult problems. That was because many POWs refused to return to their home country, or were reluctant. There were a variety of reasons. Some refused to go to their home country because they didn't want to return to military service when they got home. Some avoided repatriation because they had either helped the enemy or volunteered to be captured and feared repercussions back home. There were those troops who had been captured by the enemy, then forced into serving the enemy side, and later became POWs again by the friendly side. They definitely did not want any part of the POW exchange.
Accordingly, there were many levels of problems—personal problems, issues with principles, humanitarian issues, legal issues, the individual right to pursue happiness, forceful repatriation, and other problems associated with philosophy and ideology, which made the matter much more complicated.

The communist side often indoctrinated the POWs and conscripted them into service. Clause 118 of the Geneva Convention was not very clear in practice.

Moreover, there were many difficulties in determining the actual number of POWs. There were difficulties in defining the meaning of the POW itself.

1. <u>Definition of POW</u>

There were many civilians mixed into the POW population, not clear of their connection with the military. Also, the KPA, at the time of its occupation of Seoul, forced many students and youths into service under the name of a volunteer army. Whether they should be lumped into the POW population of the regular army was an issue.

Second, a great number of ROKA personnel were captured during the early stages of the war, and most of them had been pushed into service for KPA. They had been captured by the UN troops. So, the question was—were they North Korean POWs, even though their legal nationality was South Korean?

2. Number of POWs and Roster

The number of POWs differed each and every time the negotiating parties presented their lists. The communist side delivered inconsistent figures on a regular basis. On December 18, 1951, they listed:

- ROKA POWs : 7,142 men
- UN POWs   : 4,417 men
- Total   : 11,559 men[15]

These numbers were very far apart from the UN's account of missing troops. For instance, the total MIA's for the UN side was 188,000 men[16], whereas the communist side POW numbers amounted to less than 10% of the missing men. The UN reported that it had in custody the following number of POWs:

- PRC POWs   : 20,720 men
- KPA POWs   : 121,360 men
- Total   : 132,080 men[17]

(As a reference, my own experience during the war indicated that most of the MIA's other than those killed or wounded were POWs.)

---

[15] Hermes, Walter, *Truce Tent and Fighting Front: United States Army in the Korean War*, (Washington DC, US Army Center of Military History, 1992), p.141

[16] Ibid., p.141

[17] Ibid., p.141

US POWs

The disparity between the numbers for the POWs was unreasonable at best, and the UN rejected the communist claim, especially when the KPA had reported on the radio during its first occupation of Seoul that "we have captured 65,000 ROK POWs in the battle for Seoul."

Lee Sang-jo, a North Korean representative, explained the disparity this way: "Most of the POWs were civilians, so we released all of them at the front." He then accused the UN side of leaving out 44,259 men and 1,459 names.

The UN's Rear Admiral R.E. Libby, USN explained that 37,000 POWs have initially been South Korean civilians, and 1,600 men were released because they were civilians.

A high number of the KPA POWs had been former ROKA personnel captured and re-educated for KPA service. They had been captured by the UN.[18]

---

[18] Ibid., p.136

Considering the number of POWs housed by the UN in camps in KoJe Island and Pusan, it was clear that the communist side left them out of the roster.

So the negotiations concerning the POWs faltered, and the UNC applied more pressure on the communist side by bombing their supply routes.

3. Principles for POW Exchange/Exchange candidates

With the truce negotiations bogged down, they agreed to exchange the wounded prisoners first. On April 26, 1952, the communist side released 684 men, and the UN released 6,670 men during the first round of the POW exchange.[19]

As alluded to earlier, the Geneva Convention Article 118 says that the POWs must be returned to their home countries as soon as the hostilities terminated. During the process of sorting out the prisoners, the UN came to learn that KPA POWs were not all from North Korea. A good portion of the POWs was from the South, and that they had been ROKA personnel who later were conscripted into KPA.[20]

Those who originally hailed from the South refused to be shipped to North Korea and fought with those North Korean KPA POWs who wanted to go to North Korea. Their fights often ended up in deaths on a daily basis.

The PRC POWs were in a similar situation. Those Chinese supporters of Chiang Kaishek refused to be shipped to mainland China's communist rule.

President Truman concluded that shipping them to communist territories against their will was inhumane and he directed

---

[19] Archives, Armistice Talks in Korea (1951-1953), Russian Foreign Policy Archives, English translation, p.85

[20] Hermes, Walter, *Truce Tent, and Fighting Front: United States Army in the Korean War*, (Washington DC, US Army Center of Military History, 1992), p.142

General Ridgway to follow the principle of "voluntary repatriation" and leave the decision up to the POWs whether they wanted to go to their home countries or not.

While the UN side insisted on the voluntary repatriation, the communist side wanted to follow the all-for-all repatriation as depicted in Geneva Convention Article 118. This difference of approach caused a fierce verbal argument every day for about two years. In the end, they agreed to repatriate only those who agreed to be repatriated. For those who didn't want to be repatriated, it was decided to send them to a third country for a three-month waiting period to determine whether they wanted to be repatriated or not.

Thus, the parties settled on a new method other than what the Geneva Convention Article 118 called for. So, why did the UN side insist on the voluntary repatriation method? Here are the reasons:

- Humanitarian aspect: As pointed out earlier, the UN side held a great many KPA prisoners who were initially from the South as well as those who hated communism. The majority of them had been ROKA personnel captured in combat. They were later forced to serve KPA, then captured by the UN forces or ROKA. Being from the South, they wanted to remain in their hometown no matter what happened.
- Military aspect: There was a second reason why the UN side didn't want to repatriate the KPA prisoners who were originally from the South. If they were repatriated to the North, they would be conscripted back to service for KPA. That would be helping the KPA increase its manpower, and there was no reason for the UN side to help the enemy.

This Voluntary Repatriation strategy had a negative aspect as well. The enemies used the same argument to hold back about 80,000 ROKA POWs, stating that "they didn't want to be repatriated back to South Korea."

Retaining these many POWs was not welcomed in some circles. S.P. Suzdalev, the Soviet Ambassador to North Korea at that time, opposed the holding of so many prisoners. According to the documents retrieved from Russian Foreign Ministry Archive after the collapse of the Soviet Union, he was concerned about detaining so many prisoners and managing them. He urged returning most of the prisoners.[21]

Maybe the good Ambassador had forgotten what the Soviet Union had done to German POWs after WWII. The Soviets did not repatriate the German POWs. Instead, the Soviets marshaled all the POWs in Poland and used them to rebuild roadways and facilities.

Kim Il-sung is signing the truce agreement in Pyongyang.
July 27, 1953

---

[21] Russian Archives, "Armistice Talks" (Volokhova, 2002), p.85

Chapter 3
WHY CAN'T THE POWs GO HOME?

Why can't our POWs come home?

This may be a simple question, but it is very complicated to answer. I have spent a lot of time thinking about it and here are some reasons why it is such a complicated issue. First, I want to talk about how North Korea views our POWs.

1. DPRK's View of ROK POWs

The difference in the concept of governance and territory:

DPRK deems the entire Korean peninsula as its territory, and considers South Korea as part of DPRK.[22]

Accordingly, ROKA personnel are DPRK subjects. Therefore, those ROKA personnel who had taken up arms against DPRK were regarded as rebels, not as troops representing a foreign nation. DPRK defines the Korean War as a civil war. Further, ROKA, considered a stool pigeon for US imperialists, had interfered with the unification of the fatherland. South Korea is a reactionary element that interfered with Kim Il-sung's mission to free the southern brethren from the US imperialists. Therefore, none of the articles in the Geneva Convention

---

[22] DPRK Workers Party doctrine and Constitution. South Korea has a similar clause in its constitution.

applied to them. Articles 49 to 57 dealing with forced labor or forced conscription of prisoners of war did not apply to ROKA POWs. Nor did Article 118 which called for the immediate repatriation of POWs to their homeland. They were already in their homeland according to DPRK's argument.

DPRK Cabinet Order Number 143:

North Korea's attitude toward South Korean POWs became crystallized when North Korea's leader Kim Il-sung issued his Cabinet Order Number 143 in 1956. Basically, it lay the groundwork for North Korea to claim that "No POW exists inside North Korea." Naturally, this edict negated the presence of South Korean POWs altogether.

As I said earlier, North Korea does not regard the Korean War as a war between nations, but a civil war between Koreans. That way, the North Koreans could justify calling the US participation as the "Invasion by the US imperialists." So, the ROKA troops had been forced to serve the invaders, and the North Korean troops "liberated" the ROKA troops from the shackles of the invaders of the fatherland.

Also, because the conflict was a civil war, the ROKA troops were mere mobs of rioters, rebels, reactionary elements, or traitors, and there was no need to worry about whether they were legitimate international POWs subject to Geneva Convention and such.[23]

Rather, North Korean KPA
- forced the ROKA POWs into hard labor and treated them in the most inhumane way;
- detained 80,000 POWs at time of POW exchange;
- retrained the ROKA POWs and forced them into service in the front[24]

---

[23] DPRK signed on to the Geneva Convention in 1949.

[24] Hermes, Walter, *Truce Tent and Fighting Front: United States Army in the Korean War*, (Washington DC, US Army Center of Military History, 1992), p.142

These actions by North Korea clearly indicate that they never intended to treat the ROKA POWs as real prisoners of war in the first place. This type of mentality had led Kim Il-sung to declare Cabinet Order 143. What bothers me is that there are leftist academicians in South Korea today who subscribe to the notion that the Korean War was a civil war within the Korean peninsula. This argument provides justification for North Korea to ignore the Geneva Convention. The whole world knows that the Korean War was ideological warfare, a severe confrontation between the totalitarian communism and free capitalism.

The Korean War was a result of the collusion between Kim Il-sung, Joseph Stalin, and Mao Zedong, not at all a civil war. Because it was a confrontational war between the communist forces and the free world, it is often referred to as "proxy war" as well.

In recent years, there have been multiple contacts between the North and the South with many opportunities to present the POW issue, such as the summit between Roh Moo-hyun of the South and Kim Jong-il of the North in October 2007. When our side brought out the subject of POWs from the Korean War, the North Korean side would halt the meetings and become silent.

Agreement between Kim Il-sung and Mao Zedong Regarding the POW Issue:

North Korea have always lied that it had returned all the POWs according to their wish at the time of POW exchange according to the provisions of the truce. The documents retrieved from Russian Foreign Ministry after the collapse of the Soviet Union proved that North Korea had been lying all along.

In a letter to the Minister of Foreign Affairs Vyacheslav Molotov on December 2, 1953, Nikolai Fedorenko (Soviet Union representative to the UN Security Council) wrote about the meeting Kim Il-sung, and Mao Zedong had in Peking regarding the ROKA POWs. Fedorenko spelled out the extent of the ROKA POWs—13,094 men from Syngman Rhee's army (ROKA), 6,340 men serving KPA, and 42,262 men working in the DPRK Railroad Works Department and other service sectors. He quoted Kim Il-sung to say, "If we sent the ROKA POWs late, then they will catch our violation so I won't send them now. I will keep them in the northern region, spread them out, and keep them from running away or coming in contact with the reps from neutral nations."[25]

This document was clear proof that North Korea's claim that it had returned all the POWs has been false all along. There wasn't much that could be done about this situation, though. The US side needed to pay attention to Europe. Eastern Europe was turning communist in a hurry, threatening the existence of NATO, which had been established in 1949 to guard against the communist expansion.

2. Korean War and Global Situation (Political Landscape Inside the US)

Anti-war sentiment within the US:

As the Korean War was prolonged without much progress, anti-war sentiment began to form among the American public, since the majority of the population had never heard of a country called Korea. They questioned the merit of continuing the war. So many lives have been sacrificed.

Then-presidential candidate General Dwight Eisenhower made a campaign promise to end the Korean War and thus became the 34th President of the United States. Once elected, he directed the Fareast Command and the 8th Army to pursue a truce as soon as possible.

The talks regarding the POWs were not satisfactory, and the primary tool to persuade the enemy to fall in line was the continued pressure by using the superior air and naval operations, but Fareast Command and the 8th Army were no

---

[25] Archives, Armistice Talks in Korea (1951-1953), Documents from the Russian Foreign Policy Archives), p.89

longer in a position to maintain the pressure on the communist forces.

The NATO issue:

The European continent, devastated by two world wars, was ripe for the Communist International (Comintern) movement that promised the moon for the proletarian working class. On the surface, Comintern advocated world revolution, but in reality, it served to propagate the Soviet agenda. Joseph Stalin dissolved Comintern in 1943 to keep Roosevelt and Churchill happy, but the Soviet mission for world domination became evident. The NATO's official site describes the founding treaty as following:

"On 4 April 1949, the 12 countries signed the North Atlantic Treaty at the Departmental Auditorium in Washington D.C., the city which lends its name to the Treaty. The Treaty committed each member to share the risk, responsibilities, and benefits of collective defense – a concept at the very heart of the Alliance. In 1949, the primary aim of the Treaty was to create a pact of mutual assistance to counter the risk that the Soviet Union would seek to extend its control of Eastern Europe to other parts of the continent....

The hostilities that had characterized relations between Soviet and Western powers since 1917 gradually re-emerged at the end of the Second World War. This "East-West" divide was fuelled by conflicting interests and political ideologies. There were clashes over peace agreements and reparations, and tensions were exacerbated by events such as the Berlin blockade in April 1948, the June 1948 coup in Czechoslovakia, and direct threats to the sovereignty of Norway, Greece, and Turkey. As the power of the Soviet Union spread to several Eastern European countries, there was concern among Western European countries that Moscow would impose its ideology and authority across Europe. From the end of the Second World War in 1945, Western governments started reducing their defense establishments and demobilizing their forces. In January 1948, however, British Foreign Secretary Ernest Bevin spoke of the need for a "treaty of alliance and mutual assistance," a defensive alliance and a regional grouping within the framework of the UN Charter."[26]

It is clear, from studying what was going on in the US and Europe, that the confrontation between the Soviet-led communist movement was global in nature. The US's priority was Europe, and it couldn't afford a prolonged truce negotiation in Korea.

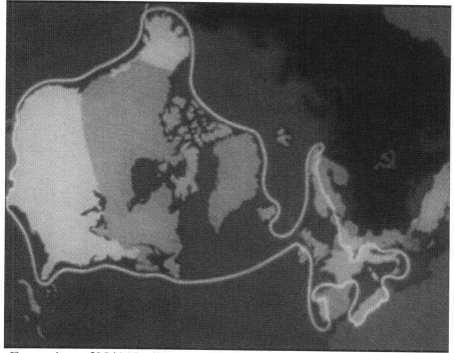

Formation of NATO alliance—North America and European nations
NATO Archive, 1949

3. <u>South Korean Perception Regarding POWs</u>

Then the next question is, what did the South Koreans think about the POW issue?

---

[26] https://www.nato.int/cps/ua/natohq/topics_67656.htm

In 2005, I had a chance to meet and talk with former South Korean Prime Minister Kang Young-hoon.[27]
We had lunch together at Plaza Hotel downtown Seoul, and I asked him why I couldn't find any recorded material on POWs who had been captured and detained in North Korea, especially concerning any effort to free them.

Kang's reply was brief. He said, "Had General Choi Duk-shin, our representative, been more aggressive about the POW exchange issue, we might have had better results."

I have read a lot of books and documents regarding the truce and the POW exchange, especially the book written by Dr. Walter G. Hermes, Truce Tent and Fighting Front: United States Army in the Korean War. I repeatedly read it, but I couldn't find any incidences of our side, be it General Paik Sun-yop or General Choi Duk-shin, raising the POW issue anywhere. The POW exchange issue came on later in the truce negotiations, and the South Korean role was significant as well.

From my conversation with Kang, all I gathered was a sense that our side did not push very hard to free our POWs. Talking to my friends who have been with the ROK Defense Department for many years, or they revealed that many personnel in the depart-ment harbored a negative attitude toward the POWs. I think this negative attitude was rooted in a notion that "a soldier should fight to the end till death, not surrender to the enemy." This view was a holdover from the Japanese philosophy which favored honorable death rather than surrender.[28]

---

[27] Former Prime Minister and General Kang Young-hoon was the team leader of the ROKA Communication Officers during the Korean War. As a communication officer, he was well versed in materials concerning strategies employed by the USFK and ROKA. During the military coup led by Park Chung-hee, he had opposed the coup and was stripped of his lieutenant general rank. I had met him in Los Angeles when he was working on his Ph.D. at USC, while I was at UCLA.

[28] Old Japanese combat manual includes a sentence, "A soldier shall maintain his honor by committing suicide rather than being captured by the enemy."

Considering that many ROKA officers were trained in Japanese military schools, it was very likely that such an attitude had been inculcated into their consciousness. Actually, the Japanese troops fought to the end in defense of Okinawa during the Pacific War until they lost most of the men, and the remaining forces took their own lives.

South Korean Public's Interest in POWs Return:

The South Korean public had no idea about the POW issue until Lieutenant Cho Chang-ho escaped from North Korea and told them, "There are many South Korean POWs detained in North Korea." I was in the Korean War, but I didn't know North Korea had been detaining South Korean soldiers all these years after the war. I always thought that all the POWs had been returned according to the terms of the truce within 60 days of the signing. I thought everyone was free to go wherever they wanted to South or North, but I never imagine that North Korea had been keeping so many South Korean POWs against their will.

I was wounded in the war and spent more than a year in the hospital. After I was honorably discharged after my treatment, I came to the United States to study, never paying attention to the problem until I saw Lieutenant Cho speak on television in 1994, forty-one years after the war was over.

According to Lieutenant Cho, he escaped to the South in 1994 when President of South Korea Kim Young-sam was in power. He was afforded a great welcome, invited to speak everywhere, schools and gatherings to talk about South Korean POWs, as well as appear on television. He appeared in documentaries that were shown in theaters everywhere.[29]

---

[29] DVD's, "Returned from Death"; "South Korean POWs Journal," produced by KBS are available. Call (323) 931-7311 or (714)717-1121; Email chungpow@hotmail.com or tombyun@yahoo.com

But the new administration led by President Kim Dae-jung in 1997 changed everything for Lieutenant Cho. The government banned all the media coverage, stopped all his lectures, and limited his outside activities with anything to do with the POW issue. Basically, he lived in a restricted state with no freedom to talk about his hellish life in North Korea.[30]

I was involved in founding The Korean POW Rescue Committee in Los Angeles in 2004 and participated in a variety of functions concerning the POW issue including sponsoring a forum in Washington DC in 2005. I was active in promoting legislation to bring the POWs home to South Korea and worked with some legislators in South Korea such as Park Geun-hye, Kim Moon-su, Hwang Jin-ha, Park Jin, and other members of the National Assembly. We also pursued the press to report the plight of the POWs, and many newspapers responded, such as Segye Ilbo, Kookmin Ilbo, DongA Ilbo, Chosun Ilbo, Joongang Ilbo, by informing the general public.

Unfortunately, the public response in South Korea was lukewarm at best. Half a century had passed since the truce was signed, and the POWs were about to disappear from the collective consciousness altogether, and the advent of the Kim Dae-jung government wanted to shy away from the issue for reasons that it interfered with their Sunshine Policy. By adopting this policy, the Kim administration sought to improve the relations between the South and the North, and they didn't want to bring up the POW issue with the North. President Kim and the Sunshine cohorts did not want to annoy and upset Pyongyang.

Besides the Sunshine cohorts, the so-called Jusapa (devotees of the Kim regime of the North) and anti-US ideologues became active in propagating the notion that the US had started the Korean War by invading the Korean peninsula. The Sunshine politics of the Kim Dae-jung administration continued with the election of Roh Moo-hyun in the presidential office. The Jusapa

---

[30] Lieutenant Cho told me about his experience in April 2005, when I accompanied him to Washington DC for the Capitol Hill Forum. He said me the same information on other occasions.

elements openly advocated anti-US sentiments, thereby characterizing the ROKA (South Korean army) efforts as a front for the US invasion and nullifying the sacrifices made by the South Korean POWs.

Professor Kang Jong-ku[31] is a representative of this Jusapa thinking. He has stated, "The Korean War was a unification war of the Korean peninsula, and the US interfered with the unification effort." He further expressed that the South Korean army was a "stool pigeon for US imperialists" as well as other propaganda-related derogatory characterization.

The ideological disparity between the Jusapa group and the public even led to a controversy surrounding General MacArthur's statue in Inchon.[32]

Looking back, the majority of the troops who had fought in the frontline face-to-face with the enemy had hailed from the poor, uneducated class in South Korea.

The Korean peninsula liberated from the shackles of imperial Japan was poverty stricken. The northern half above the 38th Parallel fell into the hands of communists. In the South, the poor population who were not accustomed to the democratic ways employed by the US military government, became very confused about democracy and how the system worked.

Furthermore, the Korean War occurred before the South Korean population had a chance to fully digest the concept of equality, due process, and the legal system associated with free democracy. In this environment, the children of high officials

---

[31] A former Sociology professor at Dongguk University and Kim Il-sung devotee. On 10/12/2005, Justice Minister Chun Jung-bae instructed the prosecution not to arrest Kang Jeong-ku, who was at the center of an ideological controversy due to his justification of North Korea's launch of the Korean War.

[32] Kirk, Donald, "Korea's generational clash," The Christian Science Monitor, 8/8 2005, https://www.csmonitor.com/2005/0808/p07s01-woap.html

and the wealthy class avoided the military service by virtue of power and money.

Hence they have become the leading class of the South Korean society without fully appreciating the ramification of the war or the POWs. Thus, chances are that the POWs were not on their priority list. This observation is supported by the fact that none of the children of the top ten conglomerates (with the exception of Hyundai) had fought in the war, or performed their military service.

In summary, with pro-North ideologues and draft dodges leading the society, it would be impossible to expect that they would pay attention to the POWs who have sacrificed their lives for their nation.

4. Did the Communists Want to Detain More POWs?

Then, why did the communists detain such a massive number of POWs by illegal means?

First, the communist leadership wanted to detain as many POWs as possible and use them as laborers for building infrastructures that were destroyed during the war, i.e., port facilities, roads, bridges, iron mining, coal mining, and other projects that required hard labor. The US Air Force destroyed everything and anything that was standing, be they military facilities, railroads, roadway, port facilities, and vehicles. North Korea's transport system was non-existent, and they had to rebuild the infrastructure in a hurry. Our POWs were used for this reconstruction effort.

According to Lieutenant Cho and other escapees following, all the POWs (other than those forced into KPA service) had been put to hard labor.[33]

---

[33] Testimonies by the former POWs who have escaped from North Korea.

KPA had experienced significant manpower loss due to the massive firepower by the US forces, and it sought to replenish the ranks with South Korean POWs.

Because KPA lost the majority of its infantrymen, the men-to-women ratio in North Korea was lopsided. This was a societal concern that needed attention. In 1956, the North Korean government issued citizenship to all the POWs and forced them into marriages.

The UN side, realizing that North Korea had detained an enormous number of POWs, requested to form an inspection team by the International Committee of the Red Cross (ICRC) to interview the POWs and make inquiries as to their intention.

But the North Korean representative Lee Sang-jo responded, "For the ICRC team to enter North Korea to interview the POWs is an excuse to spy on the military facilities. We'd rather quit the truce talks than allow the ICRC to enter North Korea."

In actuality, North Korea had the POWs working in mines scattered all over the place, or training in KPA bases, and the ICRC inspectors were sure to find them. North Korea certainly didn't want the inspectors near them.

North Korea released 13,444 men (including 8,321 ROKA troops) out of the 92,070 total. North Korea kept the remaining 78,636 men, mostly ROKA, citing that they wanted to stay. That was the biggest reason for the detainment, why they couldn't come home.

In the meantime, as the truce talks bogged down in a stalemate because of the POW issue, Joseph Stalin died in March 1953, and this changed the dynamics of the world situation. The truce talks picked up steam then. The Soviets had a different approach to the POW issue. After the WWII, they had kept the German POWs in Poland and put them to work on infrastructure. In the Fareast front, they held the Japanese prisoners and had them work in Siberia for five years before releasing them. So, they really didn't pay attention to things like the Geneva Convention. In case of the Korean War, North

Korea needed a lot of labor force after the war, and when the UN came up with voluntary repatriation, they jumped on the idea and used it to keep the POWs.

When I interviewed Lieutenant Cho and other POWs who had escaped from North Korea, I asked them tons of questions, such as, "Why didn't you return at the time of POW exchange, but waited decades before you escaped risking your life?" and "What kind of a life did you live in North Korea?"

The end result of these interviews was that they had not stayed in North Korea on their own volition. The communist side had told a lie that the POWs had chosen to remain in North Korea.

In summary, here are the reasons why I think our POWs got caught in the impossible situation, why they couldn't come home.

- The UN's principle of "voluntary repatriation" worked against us.
- The truce talks bogged down, and the US—the leading player for the UN side—had issues, domestic and international, and was not in a position to pursue to the end the false claims of the communist side.
- The ROK government and the public were not interested in the fate of our POWs.
- North Korea was determined to detain as many POWs as possible right from the beginning.

Chapter 4
TESTIMONIES BY THE POWs

The first POW who had escaped from North Korea, Lieutenant Cho Chang-ho shocked us with the information about our 78,636 POWs detained in North Korea after the war. Having accompanied him to Washington DC and Seoul for many seminars and meetings, I had spent a lot of time with Lieutenant Cho Chang-ho before he passed away in 2006 and heard a great deal about his journey from the time he joined ROKA to his escape from North Korea.

I would like to share some of his stories so the readers can get an idea what life was like for him.

Lieutenant Cho was a first-year student at Yonsei University majoring in education when the Korean War broke out. He transferred to the Army University School and received training. After two months, he received artillery training and became a gunnery officer in 1953. He was assigned to ROKA 9th Division, 2nd Battalion and served as a field artillery forward observer.

His unit suffered a surprise attack by PRC during its 5th assault. His entire unit collapsed. Lost in the hills, he wandered into a house for a drink of water. There, he was captured by the PRC troops and became a POW. As he was being transferred to North Korean custody, he attempted to escape, but he was captured by the North Korean forces. He was labeled an undesirable element and was sentenced to hard labor at the notorious Aoji coal mine.

He worked with about 500 fellow South Korean POWs and local political prisoners from within North Korea. South Korean POWs did not get a blanket, pillow, toothpaste nor toothbrush. They provided masks to local political prisoners, but not the POWs. After working in the mine for five years without a blanket or a mask in the tunnel filled with coal dust, he couldn't breathe or speak. One day after about ten years, he lost his teeth, all at once. He said he had never used a toothbrush in twelve years.

He came out of the coal mine after twelve years. The authorities arranged a marriage for him, and his bride turned out to be a South Korean woman. She had twin boys and a girl after a few years. They lived in extreme poverty, but somewhat happy. That was until the food situation deteriorated. The families of the POWs were the first ones to get their food distribution cut, gradually at first but then stopped after a while. He and his family were on their own, and they had to find food somehow. Lieutenant Cho and his two sons planted corn in the hill behind their house and barely managed to avoid starvation.

One day, his wife disappeared suddenly. She didn't come home. He finally found out that the local state security agency (SSA) had arrested her because she had failed to file the secret monthly reports to the local party official about her husband's activities.

His health worsened, owing to the lung disease from the coal dust and lack of nutrition. One day, while he was digging around the corn patch, he told his sons, "It doesn't look like I am going to last too much longer. When I die, bury me here on the sunny side. Don't write anything on the tombstone but just 'A man from the South,' that's it."

Lieutenant Cho continued, "One day in 1987, a stranger came by and asked me, 'Aren't you from the South?' I wasn't sure who or what he was, so I didn't answer him. He asked me again, 'Did you come from Seoul?' So, I just nodded without saying anything. He said he went back and forth to Seoul often and that he could deliver my message to my relatives in Seoul and asked me their address. I was suspicious of him and didn't say anything. He could have been from the SSA. He said again that he could deliver a message for me, but I stopped talking to him.

"After that, he stopped by to talk to me every time he was in the area. He kept telling me that he could deliver a message. So I thought, well, I am not going to live too much longer. Either I die by beating in the hands of the SSA agents or just die here eventually, it really didn't matter. So, I told him, 'Then get in touch with my folks,' and gave him a letter and put the picture of my mother in the letter and wrote the address of my older sister at Sungshin Women's University. My sister was a Dean at the Liberal Arts Department. The man turned out to be a broker and delivered the letter to my sister.

"She read the letter and studied the picture and determined that it was me. She followed the broker to Beijing and then to Tumen River across from Aoji. From the Chinese side of the river, they could see my house. The broker told my sister, 'If you want, I will bring him closer so you can see him.' My sister told him it was too dangerous. After that, my sister gave the broker a lot of money to smuggle me out on a boat from Dalian, China. I boarded an old wooden tug boat at night and hid in a cargo locker under the floor and traveled all night to South Korea.

"After several hours, the boat suddenly stopped. It was the South Korean Coast Guard who stopped us. They found me hiding in the locker and asked me questions. They learned that I was a POW escaping from North Korea and they turned polite suddenly. They offered to take me on the Coast Guard ship and escorted me all the way to Inchon. They checked me into a hospital for examination, and the next day, the Minister of Defense came to visit me. I was officially discharged from my unit the next day after 46 years."

Life of Isolation in North Korea

When I first met Lieutenant Cho Chang-ho in the Roof Garden Restaurant at Samil Building in Seoul in 2004, he had a hard time talking because of his lung disease. We communicated with the help of his wife. (He remarried in South Korea.)

The most challenging part of the escape was his farewell to his children in North Korea. Right before his escape, he had gathered his children and asked them to go together. But his sons told him to go by himself because it was too risky for all of them to move together. They pleaded with him to go by himself. He insisted on going together, but they were determined to send him on his own. He wanted to bring his daughter at least, but they refused. They said they would find a way to live on their own and pushed him out. They cried for a long time, and finally, he left the house.

Lieutenant Cho kept weeping as he told this story. He repeated that he had left his children behind and came down by himself. I could tell his heart was torn apart as he told his story. My heart ripped apart as well.

I asked him whether he knew what was going on during the truce negotiations. He said he had been working in the coal mine isolated from everything, then. He had no idea that the truce negotiation was going on. He had no way of knowing if there was a POW exchange, nor anything going on outside the mine. Nobody told him about the issues concerning POWs. Nobody asked him about his intention of staying in the North or going to the South.

I think the situation was the same for all the POWs. I'm sure nobody had volunteered to stay in North Korea. Also, if they assembled the POWs in one pace and asked them, "Any bastard who wants to go back to the US puppet government in the South, raise your hand now." Would anyone have raised his hand while the North Korea soldiers watched them with loaded weapons?

If anyone had volunteered to stay in North Korea on their own volition, he would have been a devoted communist, and the number would have been minimal. That was because most of the detained POWs were from the South, with all their families and relatives living in the South.

Sixty-one POWs have escaped since Lieutenant Cho's escape. Of the sixty-one POWs, ten of them passed away, and fifty-one former POWs remain at the time of this writing. All of them have their own stories. Just a few books have been published.

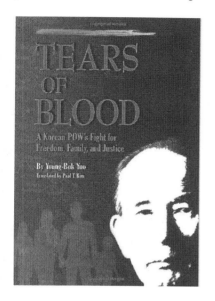

Mr. Yoo Young-bok has written a book entitled, Tears of Blood (Won Books, 2011, translated by Paul T. Kim).

Mr. Heo Jae-seok has written a book in Korean, entitled, 내이름은 똥 간나새끼였다, Nai Ereum-un Ddong Ganna saikki, My Name Was Shit Son-of-a-bitch (Won Books, 2008).

There have been a number press reports regarding these brave men in their eighties and nineties and I want to share them with the readers here.

Press Room | About | Contact

Home | Cambodia | China | Laos | North Korea | Myanmar | Tibet | Uygh

Special Reports | Multimedia | Video | Commentaries

HOME | NEWS | POLITICS

Hardly Known, Not Yet Forgotten, South Korean POWs Tell Their Story

2007-01-25

Email Comment Print

Jeon Yong-Il (L), who was taken as a war prisoner by North Korea during the Korean War, appears with Heo Pyeong-Hwan (R), Division commander of South Korea's Army 6th Infantry. Photo: AFP/Jung Yeon-Je

SEOUL—Thousands of South Koreans taken prisoner by the North during the Korean War (1950-53) were sent to do hard labor and were refused the chance to be repatriated under international law.

Those who survived the working conditions found they were still subjected to contempt and discrimination, 50 years after the end of the war.

"One day I found it rather strange that I could not hear the sound of airplanes overhead. Later, I found out the reason the skies had fallen silent: the war was over," POW Cho Chang-Ho told RFA's Korean service shortly before his death.

While 80,000 South Koreans were missing-in-action during the Korean War, only 8,000 POWs were repatriated by North Korea to the South. In contrast, 76,000 North Korean POWs were repatriated by South Korea.

Never informed

One day, my daughter came crying to me, saying that she could not get involved with a man, because she was the child of a South Korean POW. How could words describe the pain of a father?

Former POWs who managed to escape back to South Korea said that they were simply not informed that a prisoner exchange was taking place, or even that the war was over.

"At the time, I was in Manpo Prison, and I had no idea at all about the armistice or prisoner exchange," Cho said.

Another former POW, Kim Chang Seok, said: "I was captured on July 4, 1953, while on a covert mission. I didn't know about the prisoner exchange."

"After coming to South Korea, I examined relevant documents and realized that, after the end of the war, a prisoner exchange had been conducted for a couple of months. South Korean POWs in the North had no idea about the exchange when it happened. Had we known about the prisoner swap at the time, we would have done something about it," Kim told a 34-episode RFA radio documentary series titled POW Story.

The DPRK has no one to be exchanged for except those who deserted the disgraceful army and joined the people's army to fight the enemy in the past Korean War and those who came over to the North of their own accord, cursing the South Korean society.

Article 118 of the Geneva Convention on the Treatment of Prisoners of War, which came into force on Oct. 21 1950, states that: "Prisoners of war shall be released and repatriated without delay after the cessation of active hostilities."

But thousands of South Koreans were held by the other side. Their true number may never be known. North Korea still denies their existence, and many died from disease, starvation, or in industrial accidents.

Kim Kyu Hwan, a POW repatriated to the South in 2003 after performing forced labor in the Aogi mine, testified that he had worked there for 35 years.

"In North Hamgyong Province, because the coal deposit is relatively recent, the coal layers are weak, and if one digs deep, a lot of pressure develops. If the pressure is too high, the coal layers collapse, and mortal danger ensues," said Kim, whose real name has been changed at his request.

"Six hundred and seventy South Korean POWs were confined to hard labor at the Aogi coal mine in 1953, and 30 more arrived later. Out of 700 POWs, there are no more than 20 left now. Over the past five decades, many have died in working accidents, and others have died of old age," Kim said.

South Korean POWs have formally received citizenship and married North Korean women, establishing families in the North. But they have continued to be labeled as "reactionaries during the war of liberation," and are the most oppressed social category in North Korea, according to defectors whose relatives were POWs.

For example, they lacked the freedom to choose their place of work or residence, and were barred from membership in the North Korean Workers' Party.

Gruelling work

Lee Kwang Dok, nephew of Lee Ki Choon, a former POW repatriated in 2004, said his uncle was an educated man, and was sent to work in the Chungjin shipyards instead of a coal mine. Lee said his uncle lived under constant surveillance and perpetual suspicion that he might try to escape to the South Korean shore. He worked hard and lived without having any hope of ever being granted a promotion.

Oh Jeong Hwan, a POW repatriated to the South in 2000, said his sons couldn't join the North Korean army, but were forced to follow in the footsteps of their father and work in a coal mine instead.

In North Hamgyong Province, because the coal deposit is relatively recent, the coal layers are weak, and if one digs deep, a lot of pressure develops. If the pressure is too high, the coal layers collapse, and mortal danger ensues.

"One day, my daughter came crying to me, saying that she could not get involved with a man, because she was the child of a South Korean POW. How could words describe the pain of a father?" said Oh, whose name has also been changed.

"I had lived my life as a broken man since my youth, because I was a POW, and then my offspring had to dwell on this agony again, how could I not be embittered?"

POWs were not only used as forced labor. While the war was still under way, they were often given North Korean uniforms and redeployed as soldiers to fight the other side, defectors said. Some were lucky enough to be taken prisoner by the South once more, and a policy of voluntary repatriation by the South Korean and US forces after the Armistice meant that they could remain there.

Choi Hee Kyung, daughter of a deceased South Korean POW, said she decided to flee North Korea because of the perpetual discrimination and contempt she faced there.

"North Korea never treated us as human beings. Since they could not just slaughter us, they chose to use us as sheer tools devoid of any humanity. We had no future and no freedom," Choi said.

"We couldn't travel, study, or go to university, we couldn't live like human beings. Ever since I was born, until I fled North Korea, all I felt was grievance and frustration over the North Korean government's attitude toward me, and all I wanted to do was to live like a human being," she said.

Meanwhile, the remaining POWs are now into their 70s or 80s, with little time left to fulfill their lifelong dream of returning home.

Bae Young-Sook, the daughter of a deceased former POW, fulfilled her father's last wish to be buried in his hometown, and defected to South Korea carrying the urn containing her father's ashes.

"My father always said that if the two Koreas were reunified, he wanted me to visit his hometown, where fruit is plentiful and there is always enough to eat, asking me to bury whatever was left of his remains in his place of birth," she said.

"My father suffered through his entire life in North Korea and died of starvation, longing for his hometown in the South."

For its part, the North Korean government has said little about South Korean POWs under its control, essentially denying their existence.

"The South Korean authorities doggedly refuse the repatriation of unconverted long-term prisoners, calling for the 'exchange' of them for 'POWs of ROK [South Korean] army' and 'those abducted by the North,'" the official KCNA news agency said in a July 15, 1999 report.

"The DPRK has no one to be exchanged, except those who deserted the disgraceful army and joined the people's army to fight the enemy in the past Korean War and those who came over to the North of their own accord, cursing the South Korean society," it said.

Original reporting in Korean by Sookyung Lee. RFA Korean service director: Jaehoon Ahn. Translated and researched by Greg Scarlatoiu and edited by Sooil Chun. Written for the Web in English by Luisetta Mudie, and edited by Sarah Jackson-Han.

Chapter 5
WHAT HAVE WE DONE FOR OUR POWs?

Sixty years have passed since the truce was signed in 1953 following the Korean War. What has the government of South Korea done for those POWs who have spent their lives in North Korea for sixty years?

A. Efforts by South Korean Administrations

Let us do a quick review of what various administrations had done in the way of helping our POWs. The first government led by Syngman Rhee survived the communist onslaught, with the help of the UN forces. It recovered the territory as initially configured, but the war left the country in shambles. The government had no wherewithal to worry about the POWs nor had the gumption to talk to North Korea about them considering the ill feelings both sides harbored for each other.

Next, the 4.19 revolution came. The Chang Myun government's ineptness led to the military coup by Park Chung-hee, whose priorities were overcoming poverty and anti-communism policy. North Korea announced that "there will be no dialogue nor negotiation with the military dictatorship in the South." The

Park administration sought to open a dialogue with the North and dispatched Lee Hu-rak to thaw the relations. There was a rumor that Lee had brought up the POW issue, but there is no record of such discussion, so we can't know the truth.

Next, the Chun Doo-hwan government is said to have pursued improving relations despite Kim Il-sung's edict to never negotiate with the South's military dictatorship, but again there is no record of any effort to bring the POWs home. The Roh Tae-woo government did no better.

Then it was during the Kim Young-sam administration that Lieutenant Cho escaped in 1994 and brought attention to the POW issue. He was very active in the outreach effort to raise public awareness until the Kim Dae-jung government came on the scene. As I had pointed out earlier, the sunshine policy put the POW issue in the back seat or anything that would offend Kim Jong-il for that matter.

The Kim Dae-jung government simply muzzled Lieutenant Cho. Kim Dae-jung's summit with Kim Jong-il in June 2000 did not include any discussion about the men detained in the North. They issued a joint communiqué after three days of meetings, which basically espoused about Koreans getting along together. They talked about peaceful unification based on a confederation concept, the reunion of separated families, and the freeing of pro-communist prisoners in South Korea.

What was strange, Kim Dae-jung, supposedly the supreme commander of the ROK armed forces, said nothing of the troops who had been illegally detained while defending the nation. He didn't go to bat for his 78,636 subordinates in North Korea's custody, even as he was talking to Kim Jong-il. Instead, he agreed to talk about 62 longtime North Korean spies who had been in South Korean custody.[34]

---

[34] Article 3 of the Joint Communiqué—"South and North agreed to hold family reunion around August 15 and agreed to solve humanitarian problems concerning longtime spies in South Korean custody." The Kim Dae-jung government later released the 62 inmates and shipped them to North Korea.

My question is—whose president is Kim Dae-jung? I do not object to sending the 62 hardened communists to North Korea. But I do object to the fact that he kept silent about his own people, the POWs, and the abducted South Koreans. If he had not brought them up during the summit meeting held in the name of improving the South-North relations, then he must have given up his most important duty—protecting his people.

I had a chance to talk with Lee Do-soon, whose father was a South Korean POW. In the year 2000, that was, before he escaped from the North, he became very excited when he heard that South Korean president was coming. His family cheered that the South Korean president was coming to take the POWs home. They took out their best clothes and waited to greet the South Korean president.

They waited, but there was no talk about the president coming to see them. All they heard was how the president agreed to resolve the longtime spies in the South Korean custody, and they became distraught. They held each other and cried all night, thinking that there was no hope, that they were destined to die in North Korea. They felt so betrayed that if they could, they would have died.

While the families of the POWs were feeling disappointed and betrayed, then Minister of Unification Mr. Yim Dong-won thought otherwise. He had been instrumental in arranging the summit. Obviously, he thought the summit meeting was a total success and said that all those who pursued the return of the POWs while opposing the summit were warmongers. He wrote this in his memoir.[35]

From this, we can gather what the Sunshine Policy cohorts were thinking at the time. But the Sunshine era didn't last forever. Later when the North threatened to turn Seoul into "sea of fire," I couldn't help but wonder how Yim felt about the nice guys from Pyongyang. How about when they bombed

---

[35] Yim, Dong-won, Peace Maker, (Seoul, Joongang Publishing, 2008)

Yeonpyeong Island and sank the Chonan frigate? Did Mr. Yim feel that Sunshine Policy was the correct choice?

Basically, Kim Dae-jung was only interested in catering to the hereditary dictatorship, willing to ignore the sacrifices of those who had fought for the freedom of South Korea. I ask again, whose president was he?

During the next administration headed by Roh Moo-hyun, there was an attempt to bring up the discussion about the POWs and the abductee's in minister-level talks in 2006, but it didn't go anywhere. Subsequently, efforts were made to bring up the topic in minister-level talks with the North by renaming the "POWs and abductees" as "missing persons during the war," but they shot a blank on this one, too.

Toward the end of the Roh administration, Roh had a summit with Kim Jong-il in October 2007. There, he tried to bring up the subject of POWs, but Kim Jong-il and his Minister of Defence responded with silence, and the conversation about the POWs died before it started.

According to a reporter who had accompanied the presidential party to Pyongyang for the summit, "President Roh, accompanied by Kim Jang-su (South Korean Minister of Defense), raised the topic of POWs to Chairman Kim Jong-il and Choe Yong-gon (North Korean Minister of Defence), Kim Jong-il suddenly stopped talking and looked away, and the atmosphere turned cold."

On the last day of the summit, Minister Kim Jang-su asked Kim Jong-il and Choe Yong-gon, "Shouldn't we address the POW issue?" but Kim Jong-il didn't answer, just looking up at the ceiling. Minister Choe didn't say anything. That was the end of the Roh government's effort.

The reason the Roh government tried to bring up the POWs for the first time in history was due to the pressures generated, including multiple US Congressional hearings held at the Capitol Hill for the members of the House International

Relations Committee, followed by the adoption of the resolution by the Lower House.[36]

Lee Myung-bak government came next. They appeared to be very passionate about the POW problem in the beginning, but the South-North relations was icy, and the Lee government's pledge was just talk.[37]

As far as I know, the efforts mentioned above show the extent of the involvement by the South Korean government throughout the years since the truce was signed. At least the Roh government was able to bring up the topic. An ex-serviceman, Roh had an understanding of military life. Also, the external pressure from the US Congress and domestic media had prompted public discussions.

There may have been other contacts between the South and the North on the governmental level that I am not aware of, but the absence of official statements concerning POWs in numerous South-North meetings leaves me cold. I don't anticipate that this tendency will change soon.

B. Efforts by NGOs

Let me talk about an NGO I am involved with. A group of Korean War ROKA veterans got together and formed the "Korean War POW Affairs Committee" in Los Angeles in 2004 with a mission to rescue the POWs detained in North Korea.

Our first task was to confirm whether South Korean POWs were indeed detained in North Korea. If so, how many were there? Why are they held? How could we bring them home?

---

[36] H.Con.Res. 168 – 109th Congress (2005-2006) introduced by Rep. Henry Hyde on 05/26/2005; passed House 07/11/2005

[37] Mr. Hwang Jin-ha, then the Chair of the transition team for the Ministry of Defense declared in public, "The POW problem is the top priority issue for the current administration."

We read all the material issued by the Ministry of Defense. We learned that there were POWs detained in North Korea, even though we didn't know if they were alive or dead. Studying the data, we found that the numbers were different across many different documents.

Then we met the POWs who had escaped from North Korea. There were 67 escapees in 2004.[38]
We wanted to meet all of them, but we met only 6 of them in the first round.[39]

The reason was they didn't want to expose their identity in the press. The former POWs were concerned that their appearance in newspapers would put their relatives at risk of persecution in North Korea.

Here's a quick summary of what we found:
- Many South Korean POWs are detained in North Korea.
- They are very old now, unable to move freely.
- They have done hard labor while detained. Now that the POWs are old and weak, they have been released.
- Kim Il-sung's cabinet order 143 did away with their prisoner status and gave them their papers. But they were subjected to institutional discrimination. Here's what I mean by institutional discrimination. They were prohibited from joining the [North] Korean Workers Party (KWP). Their children were forbidden from going to college and military service. [40] The worst part of

---

[38] As of 2012, 87 POWs have escaped from North Korea. Of them, 60 are alive.
[39] The first meeting took place at the Garden Roof restaurant on November 18, 2004. In attendance were then National Assemblyman Kim Moon-su, Chairperson Susan Scholte from Defense Forum, Deputy Chairman Nam Shin-U from North Korea Human Rights Committee. POW escapees were: Lieutenant Cho Chang-ho, Jang Jin-hwan, Kim Dae-sung, Yu Young-bok, Park Hong-kil, Heo Jae-suk, plus two family members.
[40] According to my own research, these discriminations became

discrimination involves food distribution. When there is a shortage of food, the families of the POWs are the first ones to get cut from food distribution.

- They are under constant surveillance.
- Their children are ashamed of their lowest social status because their father is a South Korean POW.
- Nobody knows how many POWs are alive, only estimated at 100 to 500. The police probably have an accurate figure.
- Many of them are suffering from Alzheimer or physical ailments.
- American POWs are said to exist, but nobody had seen one. (Whenever I tell people that I work on the Korean War POW problem, they ask me how many American POWs there are in North Korea, so I have to be sure about this point.)
- Many POWs have been forced into service for KPA.

It was about 2005 that the Roh government was well into its term of service. They were apathetic about the POW issue because of its allegiance to the Sunshine Policy, and we decided that our committee should raise awareness about the detained POWs in North Korea. We decided we should appeal to the UN member nations that had participated in the Korean War to help us free the POWs. We decided to ask the POW escapees to help us alert the US Congress by offering their testimonies about their lives as POWs in North Korea and how they escaped.

That evening, I asked the POW gentlemen whether they would appear in a hearing in Washington DC. They lowered their heads without saying anything except Lieutenant Cho, who volunteered to give his testimony. He said, "I will come whenever you want me to. I will give my testimony any time anywhere." Another man offered to testify if he could use an alias.

---

lessened after 1980.

That was how we came to hold a forum the following year. Thanks to Susan Scholte's help, we gathered in Rayburn Hall at the Capitol Hill with so many people attending, members of the US Congress, their staff, ambassadors, diplomats, and military attaché personnel. They were all shocked to hear about the existence of South Korean POWs in North Korea. Testimonies by Lieutenant Cho and Kim Chang-sik (alias) added to their surprise. [41]

In my speech, I asked the attendees—mainly the officials from participating countries in the Korean War under UNJC—for their interest and support in bringing the ROKA POWs home. I concluded my remarks by saying, "Ladies and Gentlemen, the South Korean Army fought side by side with their allied fifteen nations led by UNC against the invasion of communism on the Korean peninsula for democracy and freedom fifty-some years ago. Our mission will never be accomplished as long as our comrades from the war are still in the hands of North Korea. A lot of non-repatriated POWs, 79,526 of them have perished. But [about] five hundred of them are still alive. These survivors are dying day by day with longing desire to go back home before they breathe their last. As a comrade-in-arms, I sincerely appeal to you to help us bring these pitiful and powerless old soldiers back home before they reach their longevity, through the United Nations since we fought the war under the United Nation's flag."

Whenever I had a chance, I told the attendees, especially the US contingents, "Would you just watch these old soldiers if they were your own?" "If we don't help them, who would help these soldiers go back home to their hometown before they die?" "It has been 52 years since the war was over, and our comrades are dying lonely."

Technically speaking, the UNC negotiators were the ones who failed the POWs by prematurely signing the armistice agreement without paying more attention to what was going on

---

[41] William Middendorf, former US Secretary of the Navy, expressed his shock and disbelief about the POWs who couldn't go home after fifty years of the truce.

back then, but I didn't belabor on that point. I just asked for their help.

The forum turned out to be a godsend, because it prompted the House of the Representatives to pass HR 168 with the help of distinguished members of the House, Representatives Edward Royce, Henry Hide, Steve Chabot, John Shimkus, Dana Rohrabacher, Joseph Pitts, Stephen Lynch, Barney Frank, Trent Franks, Ben Chandler, Christopher Smith, Jack Kingston, Danny Davis, Dan Burton, Eni Faleomavaega, Darrell Issa, Jerry Weller, Ileana Ros-Lehtinen, Joe Wilson, Michael McCaul, Michael Capuano, Ted Poe, Diane Watson, Katherine Harris, Jeff Fortenberry, Michael Honda, Luis Gutierrez, Thaddeus McCotter, James Leach, and Janice Schakowsky.

I include the bill's summary here for reference:

> "Condemns the government of the Democratic People's Republic of Korea for the abduction and continued captivity of citizens of the Republic of Korea and Japan as acts of terrorism and human rights violations.
> Calls upon the North Korean government to cease abductions, release all kidnapping victims and prisoners-of-war still alive in North Korea, and provide a full and verifiable accounting of all other cases.
> Recognizes that while the resolution of the nuclear issue with North Korea is of critical importance, U.S. officials should not be precluded from raising abduction cases and other human rights concerns in future negotiations with North Korea.
> Calls upon the U.S. government not to remove the Democratic People's Republic of Korea from the Department of State's list of State Sponsors of Terrorism until North Korea renounces state-sponsored kidnapping and provides a full accounting of all abduction cases.
> Admonishes the government of the People's Republic of China (PRC) for the forced repatriation to North Korea of Han Man-taek, a South Korean prisoner-of-war and comrade-in-arms of the United States, and for its failure to exercise sovereign control over North Korean agents operating freely within its borders."

I went to Seoul as soon as the bill passed Congress and met with then the leader of Hannara Party Assemblywoman Park Geun-hye, along with Lieutenant Cho and his wife and his classmate Colonel Lee Wan-choon. Assemblyman Hwang Jin-ha and Assemblywoman Jeon Yeo-ok were there as well. When Ms. Park saw Lieutenant Cho standing with the aid of his cane, she said, "We are so embarrassed. We should have been doing the work you are doing. You came so far." She apologized first and said, "We will do the best we can for the POW problem."

The following year, on March 24, 2006, the National Assembly of South Korea revised the law concerning "treatment of POWs" to "Repatriation of POWs and treatment law #7895" which directed the Minister of Defense to compensate the families of POW escapees from North Korea.

This law was beneficial for those family members in recovering their honor as well as finances since they had been discriminated against in North Korea. On the other hand, the members of the dominant majority party (aligned with the Roh administration) were not very interested in the POW issue. The Woori Party Assembly leaders headed by Lee Bu-young gave me excuses like, "We try our best, but it's not going well."

I requested meetings with Moon Hee-sang, then the Woori Party Chairman, but his answer was, "There is no point in meeting to talk about the POW problem. It is a difficult issue." He declined to meet and talk about it.

I was very disappointed that the ruling party was so apathetic about our heroes. Was this the price for sacrificing their lives for their nation?

We went back to Washington DC, Rayburn House Building, on April 27, 2006. This time, the trip was for a joint hearing entitled "North Korea: Human Rights Update and International Abduction Issues" before the Subcommittee on Asia and the Pacific, Subcommittee on Africa, Global Human Rights and International Operations of the Committee on International Relations.

I was very impressed by the distinguished representatives. All of them were so intent on listening to every word spoken by the witnesses.

Lieutenant Cho talked about his harrowing experiences in North Korea. Mrs. Sakie Yokota, Megumi Yokota's mother, tearfully spoke about her abducted daughter by the North Korean agents. Mr. Koh Myung-sup, a South Korean fisherman, an abductee who had escaped from North Korea also spoke.

In November 2006, our Korean POW Rescue Committee had planned to participate in exposing the POW issue at the International Human Rights Committee in Geneva, Switzerland. Lieutenant Cho had been slated to speak, but he passed away due to the lung disease.

We continued to visit with South Korean officials whenever we had a chance, but we didn't realize any progress. Time was running out on us, and we felt desperate because we saw no hope in a South-North dialogue regarding the POW problem.

Ultimately, we tried to convince the South Korean government to petition the UN, but that idea didn't go anywhere, either. We proposed to file a complaint with the International Criminal Court (ICC) in the Hague, but there was no response from the South Korean government. We talked to then Minister Hyun of Unification Ministry for two hours, but amazingly, he didn't say a word the whole time.

We did file a criminal complaint in February 2011 against the Kim Jong-il regime with charges for crimes committed against humanity, entitled, "The Factual Evidence of Human Rights Violations Committed by the North Korean Regime (DPRK, Democratic People's Republic of Korea) on Korean War POW."

In April, we filed a petition to UN Human Rights Committee to rescue the aging men. The filing process with the ICC took a whole year. Dr. Kim Han-hoi worked very hard to gather all the data and information necessary for filing the legal papers, and all of us at the POW Affairs Committee remain very grateful for his effort.

The ICC's response was not what we had expected. They said that the crimes were committed inside North Korea and that North Korea was outside their jurisdiction. Therefore, they could not conduct an investigation unless we had additional evidence that the crimes had occurred within their jurisdiction.

We replied that the POW exchange was supervised by the UNC in neutral territory at the time of the truce negotiations and that the UNC should have followed up with the exchange process in the neutral area as it had with all other POWs. The UNC did not follow up with the South Korean POWs thereby violating the human rights of the POWs.

We argued that the rights of the POWs were violated in the neutral zone, which was within the jurisdiction of the ICC. We sent the additional data and information to The Hague courts. But there was no reply.

Actually, some of our legal experts thought that the ICC might not take on our case because there was a strong possibility that they would disagree with our argument that the crimes had occurred inside the ICC jurisdiction. We asserted that the POWs had been captured in South Korea, inside the ICC jurisdiction, then abducted to North Korea, where they were detained and abused.

We hadn't heard from the Hague for a long time, and Dr. Kim, our legal counsel, went to the Hague in 2013. He found out that the ICC had replied to our emails and requested for more information and data to me.

However, I hadn't received any email from the ICC. Come to think of it, that was about the time my computer was down, unfortunately. As for the petition to UN Human Rights Committee, we haven't heard from them at all. Bottom line, I think the South Korean government must get involved to get any response from the Committee.

Chapter 6
HOW TO SOLVE THE POW PROBLEM?

Our heroes are aging as we stumble to figure out how to rescue them out of North Korea. It is painfully clear that talking to Pyongyang about freeing the gentlemen is futile. Pyongyang steadfastly promotes the ethnocentric concept of *minjok*—"Koreans for Koreans," "Brotherly solidarity," etc.—but their actions do not match their rhetoric. They even refute the existence of the POWs despite all the evidence. For this reason, some former military officers have proposed to rescue the POWs by forceful means. Let's take a look at what the South Korean government had studied up to now.

Entebbe Type Rescue Operation[42]
There have been proposals about conducting an Entebbe type raid operations using special ops personnel similar to the Israelis, but it appears unlikely.

First of all, the South Korean government would have to commit to an all-out war to carry out a rescue operation such as this, mainly when the

---

[42] "Operation Thunderbolt," or Entebbe Raid took place on July 4, 1976, at dawn. Israeli special troops rescued about 200 Israeli passengers (except for one casualty) held hostage by Palestine captors in Entebbe, Uganda.

subjects are scattered all over the country, unlike the Entebbe situation where all the victims were gathered in one place.

Also, the Entebbe operation was a result of an unwavering resolve by the government of Israel to rescue the abducted. This proposal to conduct the rescue operation for the South Korean POWs is merely wishful thinking based on emotion not hard reality.

Approaching the POW problem as "Missing in Action" Personnel[43]
Renaming our POWs as MIA in an attempt to bring up the topic with the North Korean authorities didn't fare well. The Roh administration's term came to an end, and then Minister of Unification Lee Jae-jung didn't get an opportunity to approach the North Korean authorities.

FREIKAUF Method [44]
With the advent of conservative Lee Myung-bak administration following the Roh Moo-hyun administration, South Koreans anticipated that the Lee government would be more keen on the POW issue than Roh, who had subscribed to the sunshine policies and relaxed attitude toward POWs detained in the North.

The moment the Lee administration began, the North Korean regime pressed for following up with the terms of the joint communiqué

---

[43] DPRK claimed that no POWs exist and that they and the abductees have volunteered to remain in the country. Former Minister of Unification Jung Dong-young came to an agreement at a minister-level meeting to take up the POW issue at a Red Cross meeting in November 2005. When the Red Cross meeting opened, the South Korean representative stated, "Let's discuss the abductees and the POWs." Immediately, the North Korean representative stated, "What abductees are you talking about? They all came to the North on their accord. This meeting is over," and left the meeting.

[44] From 1964 to 1989, prior to the German unification, West Germany compensated East Germany to free the political prisoners. West Germany paid 4,000 German Marks (average) per person for 33,755 prisoners and repatriated them. The total cost, including economic aid, was $2.34 billion. Interestingly, East Germany, a socialist system claiming equality, charged and received DM1,875 for laborers and DM11,250 for Ph. Ds and MDs for their freedom. ("German Ranson"—Wikipedia)

signed by Kim Dae-jung at the summit with Kim Jong-il on June 15, 2000. At the same time, the North Korean regime insisted on following up with the terms of the joint communiqué signed by Roh Moo-hyun on October 4, 2007.

Lee Myung-bak had different ideas about the agreements by the sunshine policy proponents and refused to enact the terms of the communiqués. The North stopped all communications with the South, vowing not to deal with the conservative government. Thus, there was no opportunity for the Lee government to approach the North concerning our POWs.

Meanwhile, the officials of the Ministry of Defense were discussing the Freikauf program West Germans had utilized to buy freedom for prisoners detained in East Germany. Some thought that this idea could work in the Korean situation and obtain freedom for the POWs.

I thought there were too many differences between the German and Korean situations. First, the West Germans and East Germans never fought against each other in a bitter war. Therefore, they didn't harbor the same kind of hostility for the other side as the Koreans held. POWs didn't exist for Germany.

Second, East Germany was not a dictatorship controlled entirely by a hereditary regime like North Korea. Third, Kim Il-sung had declared that no POWs existed in North Korea. It is doubtful that North Korea's current leader Kim Jong-un would know about the POWs.

The UN Route
In order to resolve the POWs problem, we need cooperation from North Korea no matter what. All things considered, it would be best for the South Korean government to approach Pyongyang in this regard.

However, the North's insistence that there were no POWs in North Korea has preempted any attempt by the South. And there does not seem to be any prospect for an opportunity shortly. That was why I thought that the UN should be involved and pushed the South Korean officials all these years to ask for UN's involvement.

To this date, I have not heard of any official request on the part of the South Korean government to solicit help from the UN. The UN had reached out to save us when the communists overran us in 1950. We needed their help the most back then, and we need their support now. I have all the reason to believe that they would help us rescue our heroes.

It is time for the government of South Korea to behave like all other developed nations that honor their heroes to the end. The US, for instance, have a policy never to abandon their soldiers, even search for the remains of their soldiers today. Could we have survived to become a prosperous nation without the heroes? What happens when we face another crisis? If we don't look after those brave souls, can we ask them to defend us next time? We must repay them for the prosperity we enjoy today.

Just as we reach out to those non-POW folks who escape from North Korea, we need to open our hearts to the POWs who still groan under oppression in the North and free them.

Chapter 7
THE POWs WHO MADE IT HOME

As of 2013, seventy-eight POWs have risked their lives and escaped from North Korea. Of them, sixty-seven gentlemen are alive. I would like to talk about how they are doing in South Korea.

South Korea's Law #7895 has been updated to include benefits for the POW escapees. It provides for their financial needs. Roughly speaking, a lower rank infantryman receives around $360,000; a non-commissioned officer, about $450,000, an officer up to $727,000. The overall average comes out to about $490,000 with free medical care.

This amount of money hardly measures up to the price they had paid with their lives, but with this, they could get by during their remaining years in comfort.

However, the reality is different from what we imagine. When they receive this money from the Ministry of Defense, it is a considerable sum of money. The problem is that the elderly gentlemen have no idea how to manage the funds, having lived in a socialist country all their life.

The money disappears quickly. In most of the cases, their relatives whom they never heard of show up at their door and ask for loans, which they never pay back. In many cases, they fall for money-making schemes and lose their shirt. Of course, when they lose all their money, nobody comes around.

All in all, they suffer the most amount of agony because of their concern for their families back in North Korea and their safety. They are always worried about that. Most of the POWs had escaped by themselves. South Korea is their home country, but they have a hard time getting adjusted to the new culture, having been away for half of a century. Their parents whom they had longed to see have passed away. And their relatives are practically strangers.

They are free from suffering hunger and maltreatment of the North, but they genuinely miss their families who they had left behind. Moreover, they indeed have a hard time adjusting to the capitalist system in their golden age after living their lives under socialism. In my conversations with the gentlemen, I found considerable dissatisfaction among them, mostly because of their confusion about the differences in the system.

For example, some of the questions they ask are: "Why doesn't the government provide a gravesite for me?" "Why do I have to pay money at the hospital?" "My grandson is going to school, and why do they ask for money?"

When I ask them, "The government gave you money for all those things. What did you do with the money?" They reply, "My relatives borrowed the money but they didn't pay back. I spent it all."

You can see how confused they are about the capitalist system. So, our heroes are having to deal with new problems as they enter the free society which they were not prepared for. Meanwhile, they long to see their family who they had left behind. They have found themselves in a unique situation in which they have to withstand the new kind of pain no humans had experienced ever before. Life is genuinely harsh for them.

EPILOGUE

War is evil. It destroys, kills, victimizes innocent people, and evaporates away human intellect and rationality. Korean War was no exception.

But when it comes to fundamental existence as in, the matter of life and death, it is only natural that we defend ourselves and our families from enemy attack. Even though the war is evil, we must be alive to be able to discuss the difference between the good and evil.

The world wars and their destruction ushered in poverty all over the world, opening the door to the vast expansion of communism. Due to limited resources, a robust and centralized system made its appearance all over the world in the name of equal distribution of resources. The communist system does not recognize private possession, controls all the production activities in the country, plans and controls all aspects of the economy. This communist system dominated half of the world and challenged free capitalism, leading to Ideological Warfare.

Koreans, liberated from the Japanese rule with the victory of the allies over Japan in the Pacific War, had little chance to celebrate the freedom they sought for thirty-five years. The Korean peninsula was cut in half across its waist by the 38th Parallel and became a battleground for the ideological war, also known as the cold war. The war began with the communist invasion of South Korea on June 25, 1950. It lasted three years and one month, producing ten million separated family members and taking more than two million lives.

Kim Il-sung's dream to turn the entire peninsula into a communist state ended as a stalemate. The war left behind hatred and mistrust between the two Koreas. In the end, the cold war ended with the collapse of the Soviet Union, but the rise of China as a new economic power caused the US to adopt strategies to keep China in check. Thus, the Korean peninsula became a battleground among the superpowers once again, dimming hopes for the prospect of unification.

If the Koreas became unified, the issues concerning POWs and abductees would be automatically solved. The massive defense spending could be used for economic development and social programs. Yet, we are still at each other's throat, wasting away human and material resources. This state of affairs tears my heart apart when I think about the future of my fatherland.

My research over the years led me to conclude that the fate of our POWs was sealed with Kim Il-sung's decision to horde them and use them as slave labor. This was documented in the Soviet Foreign Affairs archive. No wonder the North Korean truce negotiators led by Lee Sang-jo refused to have the UN inspectors to interview the POWs.

South Korea was just an observer, not an official member in the truce negotiation, and had no influence in the outcome. The anti-war mood in the US pushed the negotiators to rush the process without proper regard for the POWs detained in the North.

Kim Il-sung's subsequent declaration of "no-POWs in North Korea" prevented any possibilities for talks about their freedom, and so they were caught in obscurity on account of the cruel twists and turns of history. They are fast fading away as days go by. Are they fading away from our consciousness, too?

I ask, for whom did they toll the bell?

ABOUT THE AUTHOR

Born in Jinyoung, South Korea, Thomas Y. Chung attended the Army Officers Training School during the Korean War. He was wounded in the YangGu battle while he served ROKA 16th Regiment, 8th Division. He was discharged after spending one year in the Army hospital for medical treatment. He came to the U.S. in 1958 and attended University of Montana and California State University at Long Beach, and earned his Master's degree at Southern Illinois University. He has gone through the Ph.D. program at UCLA. He received his honorary doctorate in economics at Southern Illinois University. He is serving as the Chair of the Korean War POW Affairs, an NGO for rescuing the POWs from North Korea. He is serving as the Chair for Fareast Research Center dedicated to studying and writing about current events and economy in the Fareast region. He also serves as the Chair of the Nara Bank, co-chair of Korean American Centennial Immigration Memorial Foundation, and operates his firm, His & Her Hair Goods Co. in Los Angeles, California.

53965565R00068

Made in the USA
San Bernardino, CA
17 September 2019